Wielding the Sword of the Spirit

Treasures of Wisdom Series – Volume 2

Deborah Esther Nyamekye

© 2016 Light of the World-John8.12 Publishing
All rights reserved.
ISBN: 978-09931738-9-9

DEDICATION

I dedicate the Treasures of Wisdom Series of books to my source of revelation and inspiration, the one and only God Almighty, Creator and Redeemer through Jesus Christ the Messiah. There are no words in any language to express my profound love, gratitude, and total dependence on Him.
He is my everything!

Deborah Esther Nyamekye

CONTENTS

Preface

Chapter 1	What's in the name Jesus? Honouring the Messiah's Identity & Purpose. Poem: Jesus Christ	1
Chapter 2	Jesus is always praying & gives us reasons to Pray. Poem: A Call to Prayer: Arise!	7
Chapter 3	A Return to the "Garden" through Christ Poem: The Return	14
Chapter 4	Precious One, God Sees & Knows Poem: LOVED	21
Chapter 5	True or False Worship unto God Part 1: Cain, Abel & You – Making Choices that lead to True or False Worship unto God Part 2: Mary of Bethany, Mary Magdalene & You: No Barriers to a Worshipful Life unto God Poems: A Worshipful Life Abandoned In Worship	23
Chapter 6	"One thing" to keep the Main Thing, the Main Thing Poem: My Desire for His Things	39
Chapter 7	At the Altar of Sacrifice: What does living sacrificially for God really mean? Poem: Altar of Sacrifice	42

Chapter 8	Cultivating Harmonious Co-Existence from a Christian Perspective -The "1-2-3 Domino effect" of the Two Greatest Commandments & the Power of forgiveness Poem: Yah's Bridge of Love	46
Chapter 9	Close Friends by Divine Appointment Poem: The Spirit of Truth	52
Chapter 10	Perfect Peace like a River Poems: Receive the Master's Peace Yahweh, my Strength & Peace Peace Offering Perfect Peace	58
Chapter 11	Living a Purposeful Life unto God Poems: Significance unto Self Intimacy with Purpose	63
Chapter 12	What it means to be an Astute Businessman or Woman of God – Trusting & Immovable Poem: Trusting & Immovable	68
Chapter 13	Who I'm I? It is a Matter of Perception! Poem: The Street Dweller	73
Chapter 14	The Battle is the LORD's: True Worshippers are Guaranteed Victory in Life's Battles (2 Chronicles 20). Poem: The Battle is the LORD's	77
Chapter 15	Exaltation of Warrior God & His Chosen Warrior King, Jesus Christ Poems & Poetic Songs (Psalms): Yahweh Nissi (The LORD my Banner; Standard or Standard-Bearer) Yahweh Gibbor (Man of War; The Lord, the Mighty) Yahweh Sabaoth (The LORD of Hosts)	84

PREFACE

Wielding the Sword of the Spirit (Treasures of Wisdom Volume 2) is a collection of teachings based on diverse biblical topics about God and Jesus Christ as well as the human heart and experience presented in chapters each with inter-relating inspirational teachings and poems or poetic songs/psalms.

The inspirational teachings, packed with scriptural quotations or references are written as exhortations, devotionals, or motivational articles with counsel. In most cases the author wrote the teaching first and was inspired to write the poem that relates to the teaching soon afterwards. In some cases the poems were inspired by certain scriptures the author read or by a certain trend of thought giving the inspiration to write the teaching or exhortation derived from them.

Chapter 1
What's in the name Jesus? Honouring the Messiah's Identity & Purpose.

We are first made aware of what name the Messiah was to be called according to the will of the Most High God when the Angel appeared to Mary to tell her she was chosen by God.
In Luke 1:31-35 we read the words of the Angel as follows
"31 You will conceive and give birth to a son, and you will name him Jesus. 32 He will be very great and will be called the Son of the Most High. The Lord God will give him the throne of his ancestor David. 33 And he will reign over Israel[a] forever; his Kingdom will never end!"34 Mary asked the angel, "But how can this happen? I am a virgin." 35 The angel replied, "The Holy Spirit will come upon you, and the power of the Most High will overshadow you. So the baby to be born will be holy, and he will be called the Son of God."
As most Christians know, Jesus is the English name of the Messiah, our Lord and Saviour, who is central to our Christian Faith. Jesus is the name derived from the Latin form of the Greek name Iesous that is a rendition of the Hebrew name Yeshua which also has variants Joshua or Jeshua.

In Wikipedia we read that
-the name Yeshua is related "to the Hebrew verb root "rescue, deliver" and one of its noun forms, yešua' "deliverance"."
– "There have been various proposals as to how the literal etymological meaning of the name should be translated, including YHWH (God)saves, (is) salvation (is) a saving-cry (is) a cry-for-saving (is) a cry-for-help, (is) my help.
-Yeshua was an early Biblical Hebrew name יְהוֹשֻׁעַ Yehoshua' which underwent a shortening into later Biblical יֵשׁוּעַYeshua`, as found in certain Hebrew texts"

Isaiah (9:6) was compelled by God to tell us the identity and purpose of Jesus in this manner:
"For unto us a child is born, unto us a son is given: and the government shall be upon his shoulder: and his name shall be

called Wonderful, Counsellor, The mighty God, The everlasting Father, The Prince of Peace."

So when you say "Jesus" or "Yeshua" (God is Salvation) referring to the Messiah, you are coming in agreement with his identity and purpose as spoken by God through certain Old Testament prophets such as Isaiah.

You are also proclaiming his identity and purpose as mentioned in the New Testament as follows:

1. His oneness with God the creator. Let us remind ourselves of scriptures that speak of the fact that Jesus and God are one:

i. Jesus said (John 10:30) "I and my Father are one".

ii. Jesus referred to himself as the "I Am" when he said "Before Abraham was, I Am" (John 8:58) in the same way God did (Exodus 3:14).

When Jesus is praying for those who believe in him and says "Holy Father, keep them safe by the power of your name, the name that you gave me, so that their unity may be like ours… " (John 17:11, 21), he is in effect saying that His name is the same as God's name and this is because they are one.

iii. Jesus "who being the brightness of [his] (God's) glory, and the express image of his (God's) person…(Heb. 1:3 KJV).
iv. Jesus "Who is the image of the invisible God, the firstborn of every creature..."(Col. 1:15 KJV).

2. You agree with what the following said about Jesus:

i. The Angel Gabriel who appeared to Mary and said "31And, behold, thou shalt conceive in thy womb, and bring forth a son, and shalt call his name JESUS.32He shall be great, and shall be called the Son of the Highest: and the Lord God shall give unto him the throne of his father David:33And he shall reign over the house of Jacob forever; and of his kingdom there shall be no end." (Luke 1:31-33 KJV).

ii. The Angels who appeared to the Shepherds watching their flock:

"10And the angel said unto them, Fear not: for, behold, I bring you good tidings of great joy, which shall be to all people.11For unto you is born this day in the city of David a Saviour, which is Christ the Lord.12And this [shall be] a sign unto you; Ye shall find the babe wrapped in swaddling clothes, lying in a manger. 13And suddenly there was with the angel a multitude of the heavenly host praising God, and saying,14Glory to God in the highest, and on earth peace, good will toward men (Luke 2:10-14 KJV).

iii. Simeon a just and devout man who was "waiting for the consolation of Israel" saw Jesus and "28Then took he him up in his arms, and blessed God, and said,29Lord, now lettest thou thy servant depart in peace, according to thy word:30For mine eyes have seen thy salvation, 31Which thou hast prepared before the face of all people; 32A light to lighten the Gentiles, and the glory of thy people Israel." 34And Simeon blessed them, and said unto Mary his mother, Behold, this [child] is set for the fall and rising again of many in Israel; and for a sign which shall be spoken against;35 (Yea, a sword shall pierce through thy own soul also,) that the thoughts of many hearts may be revealed.(Luke 2:28-32,33-35 KJV).

iv. Anna the prophetess who had been fasting and praying awaiting Jesus' birth, when she saw him "gave thanks likewise unto the Lord, and spake of him to all of them that looked for redemption in Jerusalem (Luke 2:38 KJV).

v. The Magi (wise men) from the east who came to Jerusalem looking for Jesus said, "Where is he that is born King of the Jews? for we have seen his star in the east and are come to worship him." (Matt.2:2 KJV).

vi. John, an apostle of Jesus wrote:
– "In the beginning was the Word, and the Word was with God, and the Word was God.2The same was in the beginning with

God.3All things were made by him; and without him was not anything made that was made.4In him was life; and the life was the light of men.5And the light shineth in darkness; and the darkness comprehended it not.(John 1:1-5 KJV).
-He also said that Jesus is the Lamb of God who takes away the sins of the world (John 1:9).

vii. Nathanael was impressed and surprised that Jesus appeared to know him before he met Nathanael and so he said to Jesus "Rabbi, thou art the Son of God; thou art the King of Israel"(John 1:49 KJV).

viii. Peter replied to Jesus' question "Who do you say I am?" as follows "You are the Messiah, son of the living God". (Matt 16:15-16 KJV).

As we can see our Messiah's purpose and identity summed up in His name "Jesus" or "Yeshua" are expressed in scripture in various ways.

I summarise all that is mentioned as defining Jesus Christ as follows;
God's Salvation, Wonderful Counsellor, The mighty God, The everlasting Father, The Prince of Peace, The Messiah, Son of the Living God, King of Israel, Light to the Gentiles, Glory of God's people Israel, Lamb of God, the Word of God who became flesh, the awaited redeemer & consoler. A revealer of the thoughts & hearts of many as well as their rising or falling.

The significance of the name Jesus cannot be underestimated. This is why the apostle Paul wrote "8 And being found in fashion as a man, he humbled himself, and became obedient unto death, even the death of the cross. 9Wherefore God also hath highly exalted him and given him a name which is above every name: 10That at the name of Jesus every knee should bow, of [things] in heaven, and [things] in earth, and [things] under the earth;11And [that] every tongue should confess that Jesus Christ [is] Lord, to the glory of God the Father." (Phil 2:8-11 KJV).

ANOINTED ONE
Christ is the English translation of the Latin Christus and Greek Khristos from the Hebrew word (Masiah) for Messiah meaning anoint. It was used as a title for Jesus in the New Testament. Jesus was anointed. He was the one upon whom the Spirit of God descended during His baptism and identified him as the beloved, well pleasing son of God (Matt.3:17).

Jesus spoke of His purpose many times affirming that indeed "God is salvation" but I highlight here one occasion, in the temple when he quoted part of Isaiah 61 in reference to himself:

"Spirit of the Lord [is] upon me, because he hath anointed me to preach the gospel to the poor; he hath sent me to heal the brokenhearted, to preach deliverance to the captives, and recovering of sight to the blind, to set at liberty them that are bruised, preach the acceptable year of the Lord." (Luke 2:18-19 KJV).

Poem:

JESUS CHRIST

The Son of Man.
A child born unto us,
accursed for us.

A Lamb slain
with blood drained
on our sin
to set us free.

Fait accompli on a tree.

The Son of God
One with God,
given unto us.

The Way for us to
find God
know God
abide in God
become one with God.

Eternal life guaranteed.

Scriptural Inspiration: Is.9:6, John 14, 2 Corinth.5:19-21, Gal 3:13

Chapter 2
Jesus is always praying & gives us reasons to Pray

When we read about the ministry of Jesus, one thing that is clear is how he taught so much about principles of the kingdom of God and effective kingdom living through having the right attitude and heart condition before God. He would teach with direct speech, use parables or illustrations.
 A key point worth noting in relation to Jesus' ministry is the fact that God cares very much about the life of a believer in Jesus Christ beyond their salvation and is determined to ensure that we fight the good fight of faith so as to be winners in His camp or that we overcome every obstacle through the finished work at Calvary by our precious Lord and Saviour, Jesus Christ.

Jesus knew that the best way to reconcile mankind to God, even beyond salvation to a place of consistent intimacy was not only to teach about the principles and requirements of the kingdom of God but to engage with them in prayer. Prayer is communication with God by true believers in Christ who have the Holy Spirit dwelling within. The Holy Spirit is first and foremost the power of God. Without a life of communication with God in a fervent, consistent, and frequent manner, the power to sustain victorious Christian living is impossible. We can have all the teachings of the Word possible but if we do not have a relationship with the source from whom we have the Word, then we are unable to grasp the meaning of the Word. A relationship with God in the power of the Holy Spirit is cultivated through prayer and enables the Holy Spirit to teach us and consistently remind us of the teachings of Jesus.

"26I am writing these things to warn you about those who want to lead you astray. 27But you have received the Holy Spirit and he lives within you, so you don't need anyone to teach you what is true. For the Spirit teaches you everything you need to know, and what he teaches is true—it is not a lie. So just as he has taught you, remain in fellowship with Christ. (1 John 2:26-27 NLT).

"… when the Father sends the Advocate as my representative—that is, the Holy Spirit—he will teach you everything and will remind you of everything I have told you. (John 14:26 NLT). Jesus was therefore determined that believers in him then and thereafter would

1) Understand the importance of having time away from all the noise and busyness of the world to be with Abba Father.

What did he do to be our perfect example in relation to this?
In Luke 5:16 we read

"..Jesus often withdrew to the wilderness for prayer" (New Living Translation)

The New International Version of the bible states "..Jesus often withdrew to lonely places and prayed".

Also we read in Mark 1:35 "Very early in the morning, while it was still dark, Jesus got up, left the house and went off to a solitary place, where he prayed."

Based on how Jesus Christ prayed before his crucifixion revealed in the gospel of John (Chapter 17), we can conclude that when he isolated himself several times during his ministry to pray, he not only prayed for himself, but he often prayed
-for those people who would hear his teachings and believe in God through believing in who he was and his messianic mission.
-for his twelve disciples and several others who believed in him and even went from towns and villages with him such as certain women including Mary Magdalene, Joanna and Suzanna.

2) Know how to pray effectively
"The effectual fervent prayer of a righteous availeth much" (James 5:16 KJV).

Jesus took it upon himself to teach his disciples to pray
-with the right heart or motives (Matt.5:5-8)
-using the basic format as a template that pleases the Father; (Matt.5:9-13)

When we pray, we are required to
 i. recognise God as our Father who is in Heaven and hallow His name.
 ii. ask for
-God's will to be done on earth as it is in heaven
-our provision; this means we recognise him as the one we depend on for our daily needs.
-forgiveness but only if we know we have forgiven others their sins against us. This is because if we have not, then God will not forgive us our sins and non-forgiveness will serve as an obstacle to our relationship with him and therefore prevent Him from answering our prayers.
 -deliverance from temptation and evil

3) Know that
i. teaming up to pray with and for someone in their time of desperation was also required of us.

 ii. in a time of crisis, whether personal or in a group, prayer or intercession is important for it strengthens the spiritually weak.

What happened to confirm this? when Jesus retreated to the garden of Gethsemane he could have gone alone as it was the time just before the Roman Soldiers would appear with Judas to arrest him. However he did not retreat to pray on his own, he chose to asked Peter and the sons of Zebedee, namely James and John to watch and pray with him.

"36 Then Jesus went with them to the olive grove called Gethsemane, and he said, "Sit here while I go over there to pray." 37 He took Peter and Zebedee's two sons, James, and John, and he became anguished and distressed. 38 He told them, "My soul is crushed with grief to the point of death. Stay here and keep watch with me."

39 He went on a little farther and bowed with his face to the ground, praying, "My Father! If it is possible, let this cup of suffering be taken away from me. Yet I want your will to be done, not mine."40 Then he returned to the disciples and found them asleep. He said to Peter, "Couldn't you watch with me even one hour? 41 Keep watch and pray, so that you will not give in to temptation. For the spirit is willing, but the body is weak!" Then Jesus left them a second time and prayed, "My Father! If this cup cannot be taken away unless I drink it, your will be done."
43 When he returned to them again, he found them sleeping, for they couldn't keep their eyes open. 44 So he went to pray a third time, saying the same things again.45 Then he came to the disciples and said, "Go ahead and sleep. Have your rest. But look—the time has come. The Son of Man is betrayed into the hands of sinners.46 Up, let's be going. Look, my betrayer is here!" (Matt. 26:36-46NLT).

Jesus wanted his inner circle of disciples Peter, James and John with him at this time which was a period of intense spiritual warfare in the heavenly realm. Jesus knew that at that time of crisis with the hordes of hell mobilised greatly, it would be easy for them to give in to temptation such as denying they knew Jesus or reject him for fear of what people would think if they knew the disciples walked with Jesus. Therefore praying beforehand would strengthen the flesh so that it would be aligned to their willing spirit man. We know that some disciples fled after Jesus was arrested and Peter denied he knew Jesus.

Jesus knew that Peter would deny him three times and told him so (Luke 22:34), however prior to that Jesus had said to Peter (also called Simon)

"31 "Simon, Simon, Satan has asked to sift each of you like wheat. 32 But I have pleaded in prayer for you, Simon, that your faith should not fail. So when you have repented and turned to me again, strengthen your brothers." (Luke 22:31-32 NLT)

Just pause and think of how when Jesus was having his one to one with Father in a solitary place he would speak to Father about his beloved disciples and especially pray for those such as Peter he had foreknowledge would undergo affliction for his sake. That was then, but similarly Brethren, Jesus who is now seated at the right hand of Father making intercession for you and I, asking God to deliver us from evil and temptation and to bring forth His plans and purposes in our lives.

Did Simon Peter overcome? Yes, and he had a powerful ministry we read about in scripture as part of the early church apostles who were fearless preachers and miracle workers. We are also overcomers through Christ who loves us (Romans 8:37). If we have not yet seen breakthrough in certain areas of our lives, we must rest assured that it will come to pass for Father God is never late, but His timing is perfect.

Jesus not only prayed for his disciples, but he prayed "also for all who will ever believe in me through their message. 21 I pray that they will all be one, just as you and I are one—as you are in me, Father, and I am in you. And may they be in us so that the world will believe you sent me." (John 17:20-21 NLT).

It was important to Jesus that there would be unity of all believers and with God and himself. This unity would be a testimony that Jesus was sent by God. Likewise we too must pray for the unity of believers under a mission statement founded on the Word of God. Division among other things does not glorify God nor does it render His kingdom attractive to the unsaved.

Brethren, we are given insight into the mystery and power of intercessory prayer because Jesus' prayers in biblical times exemplified by John 17:20 is the reason why you and I are not only saved but we are being protected and sustained daily by the power of God. We are also more than conquerors (Romans 8:37) daily because Jesus is still making intercession for us, this time in his position as the Royal High Priest seated at the Right Hand of the Father (Romans 8:34/Eph. 8:1-6). We give him all the glory and praise!

This ought to give us assurance and hope that being a kingdom of priests seated in heavenly places with Christ, (Rev 1:6/Eph. 2:6) as we intercede for the unsaved in agreement with Jesus' prayers, they too will be saved. To God be the glory great things He has done!

Poem:

A Call to Prayer: Arise!

The mantel of prayer
is a gift to you, disciple of Christ,
not to a specific priest so accept it
as a sword to wield in the battlefield.

Firebrand!
Let the flames of prayer be released
from within to set alight Satan's plans
and to ignite the Word of truth in God's sons.

Watchman!
Look to see and hear the LORD.
Sound the alarm at the enemy's advance
upon man and with the armies of God
shoot the arrow at the hordes of hell as
a protector and defender of man.

Warrior!
As an impenetrable wall,
the LORD entreats that your prayer rain is released to fall
as fire and brimstone for the retreat of the armies of hell,
for He says
"The thief only comes to steal, kill, and destroy.
I came that they may have life, and may have it abundantly."[1]

Intercessor!
Forever seated in heavenly places
and in oneness with Spirit and Royal High Priest,
be a bridge for the crossing over into God's turf,
a mother to carry the vision unto birth and
a midwife, for the bringing forth of God's plans.

Arise!
Firebrand,
Watchman,
Warrior,
Intercessor
stand in unity on the Rock of Salvation,
your Foundation Stone who is Christ,
the Chief Cornerstone.

(Quote 1. John 10:10WEB)

Note: Prayer is communication with God. God has called us who are His to a life of prayer and in the busyness of life, it is important to remind ourselves of this every so often. In the New Testament scriptures, we are revealed the importance of prayer to Jesus Christ during his ministry. He used to frequently and consistently separate himself from the crowd and even his disciples and spend time alone with Father God. As we know there are different ways of praying to God. Prayer is not a specialised ministry only for some, so let's ensure we make prayer a lifestyle, fervently, consistently, and frequently as Jesus Christ did.

Chapter 3
A Return to the "Garden" through Christ

"A wrought-iron bench entwined with morning glories.. a rose-covered trellis… Whatever your garden is, or wherever it grows, it is yours. It is your place of solitude… It is your place of prayer and reflection…it is your place to share your time and yourself with no one but the Lord." Gena Rutherford

When I think of why Jesus came I not only get the Gospel account brought to memory but the imagery of him being the Way (encompassing his nature as the "truth and life") back to an intimate relationship with God our Creator and loving Father according to John 14:6.

Just imagine without the birth of Jesus Christ we would have absolutely no access to Father!

Jesus is the gate or Way that is narrow and unattractive, (Matthew 7:13-14) but when chosen leads to abundant and eternal life because it results in the reconciliation of mankind's relationship with Father which was lost generationally due to Adam and Eve's disobedience (Genesis 2-3)

I get the image of this process of being in Christ, walking with him "The Way" daily as being back to that place of intimacy with Abba Father, I call the "Garden". Eden was the garden in which God put Adam and Eve, He created in His image (Genesis 2).

Eden was originally a Garden where God intended to fellowship or tabernacle with His creation, Adam and Eve and their offspring forever. It was therefore meant to be a place where His creation had all they needed and a place of abundance and joy as they lived in obedience to God. However this plan of God was short lived due to Adam and Eve's disobedience to God.

The purpose for this Garden was replicated as the purpose for the tent of meeting God instructed the Israelites to build according to his specifications in the wilderness and the temple Solomon employed gifted craftsmen and builders to build for the Lord during his reign. Temples, Synagogues, and churches thereafter have been built for the purpose of worshiping God; being in the "Garden" or abodes of intimacy with Father God.

As I contemplate the abounding mercy of God which compelled Him to send Jesus as a baby born to Mary & Joseph into the World, I am reminded of the Garden of Gethsemane (Matt. 26:36) where Jesus prayed awaiting his captors who took him to be judged, humiliated, and crucified. This Garden was where we get the affirmation that Jesus Christ as the Son of Man, the last Adam was completely committed to his purpose as a life-giving spirit (1 Corinth. 15:45) through his death burial and resurrection. When Jesus said "…not my will but thine be done" (Luke 22:42 KJV), we can also read into this that He was saying "indeed I am the seed of the woman (Mary) who will crush the head of the serpent (Satan) once and for all (Gen. 3:15) to redeem mankind from sin and reconcile them back to God." This was the Merciful promise of God to Adam and Eve (Genesis 3:15) after God spoke of their punishment because of disobedience.

It is clear that God had and still has the last word in the life of mankind for while Satan thought that he had caused mankind to reject God as LORD and so master over their lives forever, God had planned even before the foundations of the earth to redeem man through the blood of the Lamb (Jesus), with which the angel Michael and heavenly hosts overcame Lucifer and his hordes during the warfare in heaven (Rev. 12).

Those who accept Jesus Christ as the Lord and Saviour God sent to the world "when the time had fully come" (Gal 4:4) receive the new birth. Their earthly bloodline connection to the first Adam which is death inducing (because the "thief" Satan is master) has been exchanged for the spiritual bloodline connection to Jesus Christ which is life-giving (John 10:10). They are heirs with Christ for the promises of God.

There are many scriptures that remind us of our intimacy with God, abiding with Him through "The Way", our Lord and Saviour Jesus Christ. These scriptures give us a picture of us being restored to the place of intimacy analogous with being restored to an intimate place "Garden" with God even before Adam and Eve sinned.

At times in scripture the earth is made to appear as one big garden with budding seeds. Our righteousness, God's doctrine, other godly ways and even God and Christ are likened to nature in some way.

In the Garden of fellowship with Abba Father,
1. As in the Garden of Gethsemane, when Jesus told his disciples not to sleep but to watch and pray with him, so too his disciples of today are called to be his prayerful watchmen, alert when the enemy comes. When we are prayerful, we are able to surrender to the will of God sacrificially as Jesus Christ did; dying with him daily we also resurrect with him in newness for the purposes of God to be fulfilled in our lives.

2. We are as the branches on the true vine (Jesus) who are pruned by the "gardener" (John 15:1 NIV) so that we would bear more fruit.

True believers in Jesus Christ have this blessed promise: "The godly shall flourish like palm trees and shall grow tall as the cedars of Lebanon. For they are transplanted into the Lord's own garden and are under his personal care. Even in old age they will still produce fruit and be vital and green" (Ps.92:12-14 TLB).

Why? He is our shelter or rock and there is no unrighteousness in Him (Ps.92:15 KJV).

3. God promises that "as the earth bringeth forth her bud, and as the garden cause the things that are down in it to spring forth; so the Lord will cause righteousness and praise to spring forth before all the nations" (Isa.61:11 NASB).

We who are the righteousness of God in Christ Jesus are the fruitful ones who personify the righteousness and praise of God springing "forth before all the nations".

In the Garden of fellowship,
-the LORD is faithful to perform His Word:
"For as the rain cometh down, and the snow from heaven, and returneth not thither, but watereth the earth, and maketh it bring forth and bud, that it may give seed to the sower, and bread to the eater:11So shall my word be that goeth forth out of my mouth: it shall not return unto me void, but it shall accomplish that which I please, and it shall prosper [in the thing] whereto I sent it." (Is.55:10-11 KJV).

- "…When we obey Him [His Word] every path He guides us on is fragrant with His loving-kindness and His truth" (Ps. 25:10 TLB).

While we stay in that place of intimacy, abiding with Father through Christ, our hearts are to Him as a garden, a place where He tabernacles.

At times, we may feel malnourished or dry, but as there are seasons of life and a time for everything (Ecc.3:1-2) so too in our lives there is the same. "He has made everything beautiful in its time… " (Ecc.3:11 NIV) and to manifest in His appointed.

God uses people as His vessels to nurture us in our Christian faith. They plant and water the Word of God in our hearts, His "Garden" through discipleship, however as the apostle Paul said on this subject to the Corinthian believers "…it was God, not we [himself & fellow minister] who made the garden grow in your hearts" (1 Corinth.3:6 TLB).

Indeed this is God's promise to us:

"The Lord will guide you continually and satisfy you with all good things…and you will be like a well-watered garden, like an ever-flowing spring" (Is. 58:11 TLB).

Dear Father,

I love you, I appreciate you, I revere you! You are all I have and all I desire. Father thank you for setting me apart as a holy vessel to glorify you. I am your holy habitation, or should I say I have become so, as you the Potter re-made me, the clay when I was born again so that I changed masters. You said to the Israelites "Let them make me a Sanctuary that I may dwell among them".(Exodus 25:8). Father as you dwelt in the sanctuary of old, so I daily offer my spirit, soul and body as your tabernacle, your sanctuary so that you may dwell in me LORD.

As you showed Moses the design of the Tabernacle while he was with you for 40 days on Mount Sinai (Ex.24:18) and you repetitively told Israel to build it to your specification (Ex. 39:42), so too I offer up my spiritual ears and eyes to you that I may daily hear your instructions and see the "designs" concerning my life so that I will live my life according to your precise specifications. In this way I will remain a mature and resourceful instrument of righteousness or be "like a well-watered Garden, like an ever flowing spring" (Is. 58:11) for your use.

Thank you Father for instructing me to separate from all uncleanliness (deception) by your leading (Is.52:10-12). Help me to live in obedience as it is my desire to abide in your presence. I also acknowledge that I can only depend on you in the power of the Holy Spirit to sustain me in the Garden of intimacy as I journey through life.

I pray in the mighty name of Jesus who made this journey possible Amen.

Poem:

The Return

I longed to return to the Garden
where man walked with His Maker
in the cool of day
so he found his way.

I longed to return to the Bosom
of Abba Father
cradled far away from the prey,
no more to stray.

He heard me and with His rod and staff
led me into His Garden paths of righteousness.

So I returned from perilous places I tread,
singing "Hallelujah, I am free from captors I dread!"

My return is as sweet as "milk and honey" in a land of plenty.
In this place, the shelter of the Most High God,
I dwell forever and gaze
upon His beauty.

Deborah Esther Nyamekye

I am protected and exalted
above my enemies.

I am blessed and highly
favoured.

"…I will offer in his tent sacrifices with shouts of joy;
I will sing and make melody to the LORD"[1]

Scriptural inspiration: Quote 1: Psalm 27:6 ESV
Genesis 1-2, Exodus 33:3, Psalms 23, 27:4-6, 91

Chapter 4
Precious One, God Sees & Knows

God knows that at times we struggle and wonder why other people seem to be getting breakthroughs at the drop of a hat so to speak. However we feel that God's promises are beyond our reach or that our prayers are not being answered. But remember you and I are equally in God's mind and so equally important to Him. In addition each and every one of us although loved by God equally is unique; fearfully and wonderfully made uniquely!

The "specifications" or strategic and creative design of God used to build my life differ entirely from that used to build another's but those "specifications" came from the same master architect, craftsman or creator, the one and only Most High God! Is that not awesome?!

What seems to be delay is not denial. In fact delay as we may define how long a promise, request or desire is being fulfilled by God is actually the amount of time God needs to work out that situation and produce His perfect outcome.

This is because He alone knows us better than we know ourselves and He alone knows the underlying issues related to that situation which we are often blind to unless He chooses to reveal them to us.

Our God knows the end from the beginning. He is all-knowing and all-seeing therefore let us trust Him one hundred percent by exercising the fruit of patience and perseverance.

While we wait on Him, let us celebrate the successes and victories of our brethren in the LORD and encourage those who are struggling whatever situation we are in whether in good or bad times, praising Him all the way!

"And let us not be weary in well doing: for in due season we shall reap, if we faint not." (Galatians 6:9 KJV).

"Wait on the LORD: be of good courage, and he shall strengthen thine heart: wait, I say, on the LORD." (Psalm 27:14)

Love the unique and beautiful you, whatever your race, nationality or whether you are rich or poor in worldly terms for in Christ you are RICH and you have what money cannot buy!

Poem:

LOVED

L-ooking at creation is as through binoculars with many views

O-f a world

V-aried, with many species, races, tribes, colours and hues.

E-xpressions of the only master of creation; a skilled architect and

excellent sculptor, reflecting His divine truths.

D-on't forget, you are precious within those many views for

"...God is Love[1]"

Scriptural inspiration: Biblical book of Genesis. Quote 1: 1 John 4:8

Chapter 5
True or False Worship unto God

Part 1: Cain, Abel & You – Making choices that lead to True or False Worship unto God.

Reference: Genesis 4 - Cain & Abel

Even though Adam and Eve sinned by disobeying God and thus caused the generational sinful nature in mankind to take root, we are presented with a situation that surprises many people who read the account of Genesis chapter 4. Cain and Abel, Adam and Eve's offspring each gave an offering to God. Adam and Eve must have taught their two sons to live a covenanted life unto God, even though they still inherited the generational sinful nature from their parents.
As long as we acknowledge we are in covenant with God which Cain and Abel did by giving God an offering, then in God's eyes we confess Him before men, and we are therefore inheritors of His promises. This fact was true in the time of Cain and Abel, throughout ancient history and is true now. God is the same yesterday, today and forever more!

As Cain and Abel acknowledged that they were God's, God expected them to also know what kind of offering He would expect and accept from them. Cain was a farmer "tiller of the ground" and he brought an offering from the land to the Lord. It was an ordinary offering. He did not give his best. This shows a lack of reverence and respect for God, so what was the result? The King James version states that God "unto Cain and to his offering he did not respect" (Gen. 4:5). This verse reminds me of the verses in Matthew 10 in the New Testament which states that Jesus will confess before his Father those who confess him before men (vs 32) and will deny before his Father those who deny him before men (vs 33).
Brethren, the truth is that we get as much out of our covenant

relationship with God as we put into it. This has not changed even since the days of Adam and Eve and their offspring, Cain, and Abel. If I say I am one who offers my life as a living sacrifice to God, but I choose to disrespect or deny God, it does not affect or change the fact that He is God nor does it prevent Him from doing His works. However I will suffer the consequences of my sins against Him which is eternal damnation unless I repent.

God chose me for salvation; therefore I should see this as a privilege and be humbled to be called His child. I should in no way expect Him to feel He is blessed to have me as His child and therefore He should do what I demand. If I do, then I am being prideful. God resists the proud and gives grace to the humble (James 4:6). I may not be having this expectation consciously but my actions towards God speaks louder than my words. I cannot hide my motives or intentions from Him for He is God and all knowing. This is expressed in David's counsel to his son which we should also live by:

"And Solomon, my son, learn to know the God of your ancestors intimately. Worship and serve him with your whole heart and a willing mind. For the LORD sees every heart and knows every plan and thought. If you seek him, you will find him. But if you forsake him, he will reject you forever" (1 Chron. 28:9 NLT).

In addition, I should not take God for granted as Cain did. Cain had free will and chose to exercise it by serving God, but he did not give his best. Assessing what this means, we can conclude that Cain was lukewarm in his approach and attitude towards God. Is God looking for lukewarm worshippers? No! He is looking for those who will be true worshippers by obeying the two greatest commandments upon which all the other eight hang (Matt. 22:36-40).

"...love the Lord thy God with all thy heart, and with all thy soul, and with all thy strength, and with all thy mind; and thy neighbour as thyself." (Luke 10:27 KJV).

The Ten Commandments enabled the people of Israel to know right from wrong. Although in Cain and Abel's time the commandments as we know them were not in existence then, the expectation of God from them is the same as it was from Israel when God gave them the Ten Commandments. This is because anyone who says they belong to God are expected by Him to exercise their free will and moral consciousness by choosing to do what is right by Him or according to His Word.

Cain did not love God wholeheartedly hence the choice to give Him an offering which reflected this fact. You only know what it is to love when you live cultivating a love relationship with God. This is true worship and from this position you learn to love yourself the way God loves you and you can therefore love others in the same way. Cain did not love God, nor himself and therefore he could not love his brother Abel.

Jesus during his ministry spoke as follows:

"23 But the time is coming—indeed it's here now—when true worshipers will worship the Father in spirit and in truth. The Father is looking for those who will worship him that way. 24 For God is Spirit, so those who worship him must worship in spirit and in truth" (John 4:23-24 NLT).

True worshippers are people who live in the Spirit or surrendered to the Holy Spirit and abide by the truth of the Word of God. They exercise their free will by making choices to the glory of God and His Kingdom. The LORD alone can judge who is a true worshipper for He looks at the heart whereas man looks at the appearance (1 Samuel 16:7).

Cain did not anticipate the consequences of this lukewarmness and disrespect towards God this is why he was very upset and "his countenance fell" (4: 6) when God did not accept his offering. He felt God should accept his offering despite it being inferior to what God expected from him. This is because Cain had no reverence for God. Friends, if you have reverence for Almighty God, you will give Him your best in relation to your time, your finances and service. After all, God is the one who not only created you, but ensures you have provision and sustains you daily.

Some people think they can take God's mercy for granted and get away with it, to the point that they say "I will sin in this way and repent later, after all the bible says if I confess my sins God is faithful and will forgive me". There are some who profess to live holy lives but only deceive men because God knows the hidden state of a man's heart; for instance they may be part of the worship team in church but are fornicating or committing adultery in secret. It is not a secret to God, for their sins are laid bare before Him who is all seeing and all knowing.

These same people being born again and therefore covenanted children of God have chosen to live lives compromising with the world and so they do not give of themselves wholeheartedly to God. However as Cain (Gen 4:6) they get very upset, and their countenance falls when God does not answer their prayers, or they do not experience breakthrough in certain areas of their lives despite supposedly seeking God for years. Could it be that God has rejected their offering of false and abominable worship which rises as a stench to His nostrils rather than sweet smelling incense as true wholehearted worship does?

This example is one of several ways believers in Jesus Christ dismiss or relegate him and God to the bottom of their list of priorities while outwardly appearing holy before men and even manage to deceive themselves that they are not doing anything wrong. Furthermore, believers in Jesus Christ have given excuses when they disobey God or engage in sin blaming the devil or saying "I am only human" with the same lips they confess "I can do all things through Christ who strengthens me" (Phil 4:13) or "I am more than a conqueror through him (Jesus) who loves me" (Romans 8:37) so if they know they have the inner strength through Christ to overcome temptation how come they have a habit of picking and choosing when to obey God and when not to?

One might make the following excuses for Cain:
• He was the offspring of Adam and therefore the adamic sin nature was raging within him as a generational iniquity, so it was easier for him to disobey God than to obey Him as it was for Adam and Eve.

• He was very upset because he did not think he had done anything against God and this is understandable because the power of iniquity of separation from God (parental sin) was such that his natural inclination was not towards pleasing God but self and Satan.

Did God give Cain these excuses in the bible? He did not and would have if they applied. Unlike Cain, Abel, Cain's brother from the same mother and father chose to please God by acknowledging God's worth as being so great that He merited Abel's best offering from his livestock. We can see that while one son of Adam (Abel) chose to do what was pleasing to God, the other (Cain) chose not to even though they both have the generational iniquity of the Adamic sin nature. Why is it that the excuses one can make for Cain's attitude towards God did not result in Abel acting in the same way as Cain did towards God?

Abel was able to make a conscious choice to give God the best of his livestock even when one would easily have thought it would have been unlikely. Another reason one may have expected Abel to not give God his best offering in addition to the aforementioned excuses for Cain's failure was because as Cain, he was a first-generation offspring of Adam and one would think greatly prone to the serpent's influence against God as his mother and father.

When we are God's, He expects us to rise above the tendency to either give in to sin or make excuses for committing recurring sin because of the generational adamic sin nature or sins of our parents and ancestors as well as our own past repetitive sins. While in covenant with God, if we can make a choice to give ourselves as living sacrifices unto God as Cain and Abel demonstrated by giving Him an offering, we can also make a choice as to what level of worship we are willing to give God while in covenant with Him; We can profess we are Christians but live as the unsaved (which is not worship at all), be in halfhearted obedience, which means lukewarmness or compromise with the world (this is also not worship) or wholehearted worship because we love Him with all our hearts, minds and souls (this is true worship).

Brethren, the point I am making is that choices to be God's children and the level of worship we give Him can be made

without fearing we will fail in our walk with God because of the Adamic sin nature, ancestral generational weaknesses or our own recurring sins of the past. God is always with those who are His to protect, strengthen and warn us of impending danger, as in the case of Cain:
"7 You will be accepted if you do what is right. But if you refuse to do what is right, then watch out! Sin is crouching at the door, eager to control you. But you must subdue it and be its master." (Gen 4:7NLT).

Even though these were times well before laws and commands were given by God to people who were covenanted with Him as we know from scripture, Genesis 4:7 lays out God's expectation of His creation who acknowledged Him as their LORD as well as the consequences for not fulfilling those expectations and what they must do to overcome sin.

Man has a moral conscience and free will and therefore has the God given ability to make choices as to whether to do the right or wrong thing. What is right or wrong according to God is knowledgeable from God's Word and directly from God by revelation or His spoken word, for instance God spoke clearly to Cain in Genesis 4:7. It is also discernment or a knowing, rooted in intuition which is supernaturally given to covenanted children of God. God therefore expected Cain and Abel to exercise their free will by choosing to give their offering to God based on what they knew to be pleasing to God and not pleasing to them.

If one says they accept their covenant relationship with God, then His expectation is that one would exercise their free will by choosing morally to do what pleases God. However, God does not give up on us; He gives us a chance to repent and change our ways as well as cautions and warns us about the consequences of continuing in sinful ways.

God demonstrated to Cain that He loved him by showing mercy to him as He did many centuries later to His covenanted children of Israel and those through Jesus Christ. God showed mercy by counseling and warning Cain (Gen 4:7) when God saw how upset he was that God rejected his offering. God did not take Cain's free will from him as He never does, but as a loving Father, His words (Gen 4:7) were to make Cain realize that the consequences of not doing the right thing would lead to "sin" not just being at his "door" but entering and taking over his life. This warning came with what Cain was to do to overcome which was to "subdue it and be its master". Sadly Cain did not heed to God's warning to subdue and master sin and instead engaged in the act of killing his brother Abel (Gen 4:8).

Brethren, it is true that as Cain & Abel, we too have generational iniquities to contend with, but as God was with Cain and Abel, so He is with us and as them, we also have what it takes to sustain a life of true worship. We are also in a better place than they were in that we have the power of God through the blood of Christ Jesus to overcome (Luke 10:18-19, Romans 8:37) Satan and his demonic powers over our bloodline. We only have to believe it, declare it and live a life abiding in Christ wholeheartedly in true worship of God as an expression of our love for Him. We also have the Holy Spirit within to convict us of sin and enable us to discern what is of God, Satan, or self. This is why we must consciously live a life abiding in God through bible study/meditation, prayer and singing praises to Him.

Yes, it is true that we all have generational iniquities and sins passed down, and Satan does not relent to attack us even when we accept Jesus Christ as Lord and Saviour but we also have a God given conscience, free will and so the ability to make choices as to whether to serve God with all our hearts, minds and souls or do so grudgingly or half-heartedly. Therefore if we say we are truly born again then our degree of victorious Christian living as worshippers of God is determined by the choices we make and not by Satan or anyone else and this is because:
"By his divine power, God has given us everything we need for living a godly life. We have received all of this by coming to know him, the one who called us to himself by means of his marvelous glory and excellence" (2 Peter 1:3)

Part 2: Mary of Bethany, Mary Magdalene & You - No barriers to a Worshipful life unto God.

MARY OF BETHANY

Mary of Bethany's unconditional love for Jesus Christ is revealed by the fact that she took advantage of opportunities when he was around to express her devotion or worship of him. The two opportunities revealed in the bible are when Mary met Jesus at

1. Martha, her sister's home (Luke 10).

While at Martha's home, Mary sat at Jesus' feet and listened to what he had to say while her sister was busy serving. Martha criticised Mary openly to Jesus, but he defended and commended her as follows:

"38 Now it came to pass, as they went, that he entered into a certain village: and a certain woman named Martha received him into her house.39 And she had a sister called Mary, which also sat at Jesus' feet, and heard his word.40 But Martha was cumbered about much serving, and came to him, and said, Lord, dost thou not care that my sister hath left me to serve alone? bid her therefore that she help me.41 And Jesus answered and said unto her, Martha, Martha, thou art careful and troubled about many things:42 But one thing is needful: and Mary hath chosen that good part, which shall not be taken away from her."(Luke 10:38-42 KJV).

2. Simon the Leper's home with her sister Martha and brother Lazarus present. (John 12). While Mary's sister Martha was serving, instead of helping as when Jesus was with them in Martha's home (see point 1) Mary gave Jesus her undivided attention and took "...a pound of ointment of spikenard, very costly, and anointed the feet of Jesus, and wiped his feet with her

hair: and the house was filled with the odour of the ointment" (John 12:3 KJV).

Judas Iscariot criticised her, again Jesus defended and commended Mary: "4 Then saith one of his disciples, Judas Iscariot, Simon's son, which should betray him, 5 Why was not this ointment sold for three hundred pence, and given to the poor? 6 This he said, not that he cared for the poor; but because he was a thief, and had the bag, and bare what was put therein.7 Then said Jesus, Let her alone: against the day of my burying hath she kept this.8 For the poor always ye have with you; but me ye have not always." (John 12:4-8 KJV).

In the biblical book of Luke, the apostle Luke writes about how the host criticised Jesus for allowing Mary to touch him:

"39 Now when the Pharisee which had bidden him saw it, he spake within himself, saying, This man, if he were a prophet, would have known who and what manner of woman this is that toucheth him: for she is a sinner.40 And Jesus answering said unto him, Simon, I have somewhat to say unto thee. And he saith, Master, say on.41 There was a certain creditor which had two debtors: the one owed five hundred pence, and the other fifty.42 And when they had nothing to pay, he frankly forgave them both. Tell me therefore, which of them will love him most?43 Simon answered and said, I suppose that he, to whom he forgave most. And he said unto him, Thou hast rightly judged.44 And he turned to the woman, and said unto Simon, Seest thou this woman? I entered into thine house, thou gavest me no water for my feet: but she hath washed my feet with tears and wiped them with the hairs of her head.

45 Thou gavest me no kiss: but this woman since the time I came in hath not ceased to kiss my feet.46 My head with oil thou didst not anoint: but this woman hath anointed my feet with ointment.47

Wherefore I say unto thee, Her sins, which are many, are forgiven; for she loved much: but to whom little is forgiven, the same loveth little.48 And he said unto her, Thy sins are forgiven.49 And they that sat at meat with him began to say within themselves, Who is this that forgiveth sins also?50 And he said to the woman, Thy faith hath saved thee; go in peace. (Luke 7:39-50 KJV).

Why did Mary of Bethany relate to Jesus in this way? As a woman who had turned her back on her life of sin (Luke in chapter 7, states that she had lived a sinful life in that town, in addition to the host's words noted above in the same chapter), believing that she had been forgiven are many sins, she felt compelled to express her gratitude in a very lovable focused manner and did not let the possibility that she might be criticised openly or secretly stop her. The purchase of expensive ointment to anoint Jesus' feet was an expression of the magnitude of her gratitude and therefore worshipful life towards Christ.

MARY MAGDALENE

Mary Magdalene was also as Mary of Bethany, completely devoted to Jesus in the manner of a true worshipper. Similar to Mary of Bethany, her total devotion and expressive worship was borne out of gratitude for what Jesus had done for her. Mary Magdalene had seven demons cast out of her by Jesus. Mary Magdalene was

-at Jesus' crucifixion (John 19:25) with other women, Jesus' mother Mary and her sister Mary, the wife of Clopas.
-the first to go to Jesus' tomb and found it empty (John 20:1-3, Mark 16:9-11).

Furthermore we know from scripture that Jesus went from town to village with his twelve disciples proclaiming the good news of the Kingdom and some women who had been delivered from infirmities were with him (Luke 8:1-3). Mary Magdalene was one of them, although Mary of Bethany was not mentioned in the Apostle Luke's account, she was likely to have been one of them.

I can imagine the women being criticised by onlookers because it was not a woman's place in that era to be taught by men or Rabbis (teachers) such as Jesus nor was it their place to follow a man around as they did. Indeed, these were bold women who were fixed on the lover of their souls Jesus, regardless of the traditions of the day. They were not only interested in learning from him, but they also wanted Jesus to reach as many people as possible with the message of the Kingdom of God and so gave from their own means to support (Luke 8:3) him and his disciples in ministry; Oh! what a great expression of love and devotion towards Jesus Christ and his God given mission!

Friends, as we can see Mary of Bethany and Mary Magdalene had Jesus on their minds and expressed their devotion to him during his ministry until he left the earth. How much more should we not be expected to live even more worshipful lives unto God than these women, for we have Jesus with us every day because of the Holy Spirit within us who testifies of Jesus and bears witness with our spirits that we are children of God (Romans 8:16). Our daily actions will also reveal to the world whether we are true worshippers all the time, some of the time or not at all.

As we know, we do not have to be standing in front of people singing or playing an instrument for God's glory to be called true worshippers of God. Anyone who accepts Jesus Christ as their Lord and Saviour (Romans 10:9-10/John 4) is born again, declared righteous and therefore has the potential to be a true worshipper. It is the outworking of this declaration that takes time. The degree of victorious fulfilment of our calling as true worshipers, worshiping God in Spirit (God's Spirit) and in Truth (God's truth) is dependent on the degree in which we abide in God or Christ through the Word (bible), prayer and praise.

Abiding in God also includes partnering with Him so that God uses us to be a blessing to the Body of Christ and to anyone or groups of people in our workplace or wherever we might be. It also includes basically thinking and focus on God from the time we wake up until we go to sleep. We may have time set aside during the day to do some bible study and pray as well, but we do not have to wait for these set times because even in our thoughts and during short pauses of a few minutes as we do our work, go shopping or whatever we are doing, we can pray and sing praises to God. Relating to God in this way shows that we acknowledge His omnipresence and live in the realm of His presence as true worshipers.

The New Covenant of Jesus Christ fulfils the covenant promise of God to the nation of Israel (Jeremiah 31:31-34), extended to all mankind regardless of their nationality or race if they are believers in Jesus:

"31Behold, the days come, saith the LORD, that I will make a new covenant with the house of Israel, and with the house of Judah:
32Not according to the covenant that I made with their fathers in the day [that] I took them by the hand to bring them out of the land of Egypt; which my covenant they brake, although I was an husband unto them, saith the LORD:
33But this [shall be] the covenant that I will make with the house of Israel; After those days, saith the LORD, I will put my law in their inward parts, and write it in their hearts; and will be their God, and they shall be my people. 34And they shall teach no more every man his neighbour, and every man his brother, saying, Know the LORD: for they shall all know me, from the least of them unto the greatest of them, saith the LORD: for I will forgive their iniquity, and I will remember their sin no more." (Jer. 31:31-34 KJV).

"26For ye are all the children of God by faith in Christ Jesus. 27For as many of you as have been baptized into Christ have put on Christ. 28There is neither Jew nor Greek, there is neither bond nor free, there is neither male nor female: for ye are all one in Christ Jesus. 29And if ye [be] Christ's, then are ye Abraham's seed, and heirs according to the promise." (Gal. 3:28-29 KJV).

While we have pastors and teachers given to us by God, there are also deceptive ones or those who are selective in what they teach so as not to become unpopular while preventing disciples from attaining the fullness of the "meat" of the Word of God. Those who depend first and foremost on what their pastors or other teachers teach them, must take note that the verses of Jeremiah 31:31-34 are in actual fact stating that through Jesus Christ in the power of the indwelling Holy Spirit who is a testimony of Jesus, you are able to receive the Word of God planted in your heart without anyone teaching you. What is required is that you partner with God for the planting of His Word in your heart by reading and studying the bible to show yourself approved unto God (2 Tim 2:15), while staying in fellowship with the Holy Spirit.

To reiterate this point in 1 John 2:26-27, John the Apostle explains that the Holy Spirit or anointing of God indwelling believers in Christ will teach them, so that they do not need anyone to teach them.

This means that you can live a life consistently as a true worshipper of God! If you cultivate a lifestyle of abiding in God and depend on Him for revelation and insight from His Word, it is unlikely that anyone can deceive you in relation to Christian doctrine or in other ways. This is because you are living as a true worshiper through fellowship with the Holy Spirit, who knows the mind and will of God and reveals it to us (1 Corinth.2:10). Remember God is Spirit, and those who worship Him must worship Him in Spirit and in Truth (John 4).

Brethren, we ought to praise God every day for His Holy Spirit, a great teacher (John 14:26) and helper who reminds us of Jesus' teachings and reveals the will of God to us directly from Him or through His Word. As you can see our victorious lives as true worshipers depends on how we relate to God and nothing else not even our church traditions or how our family related to God as we grew up from childhood to adulthood. This point is best illustrated by Jesus' conversation with the Samaritan woman he deliberately met at the well on the appointed day of her salvation, or her call to be a true worshiper.

The Samaritan woman said to Jesus "20 Our fathers worshipped in this mountain; and ye say, that in Jerusalem is the place where men ought to worship.21 Jesus saith unto her, Woman, believe me, the hour cometh, when ye shall neither in this mountain, nor yet at Jerusalem, worship the Father.22 Ye worship ye know not what: we know what we worship: for salvation is of the Jews.23 But the hour cometh, and now is, when the true worshippers shall worship the Father in spirit and in truth: for the Father seeketh such to worship him.24 God is a Spirit: and they that worship him must worship him in spirit and in truth.25 The woman saith unto him, I know that Messias cometh, which is called Christ: when he is come, he will tell us all things.26 Jesus saith unto her, I that speak unto thee am he" (John 4:20-26 KJV).

Jesus was in effect saying to the Samaritan woman that while salvation came to the world through the Jews, being a true worshiper of God was not determined or gauged by whether one worshiped upon a mountain or in Jerusalem. In other words a traditional or ancestral place of worship is not of significance, what is of significance is the state of one's heart condition before God. In other words you are not confirmed a true worshiper in God's eyes, solely because of either of the following:

-you have been a Christian all your life and have therefore been known to worship God and
-you come from a long line of Christian ancestors including your parents.

As a result of either one of the above two points, you have worshiped God in a certain way or through a particular denomination.

True worshipers are those who have a relationship with the Holy Spirit because God is Spirit, and it is only when we are in fellowship with His Holy Spirit that we can know His will, ways and truth so as to live by them. Living according to the truth of His spoken or written word equates being a true worshiper. You may have the tendency to be in likeness to either Mary Magdalene or

Mary of Bethany in terms of your completely surrendered and devoted life to God, but in a way that other Christians would appear not to understand, and so criticise you, saying 'there he/she goes again, so over the top!' Do they know what God has delivered you from so that you live with such intense love for Him through the Lord Jesus Christ? If they did, they may refrain from their criticism, but then again, they may not. Martha knew of the kind of life her sister, Mary of Bethany had been delivered from, and Judas Iscariot also knew of Mary's past life, but it did not stop them criticising her actions.

Brethren, you do not have to justify yourself or explain at length as to why you live your life the way you do unless you are giving a testimony of how God transformed your life. God will defend and commend you as He did Mary of Bethany should people criticise you openly or in their hearts as you ascribe worship to God by expressing devotion to Him wholeheartedly because you love the Lord your God with all your heart, soul and mind as we are commanded to do (Matthew 22:37).

Indeed if your heart is pure and your worship is genuine the fruit of your "love in action" or labour for God's sake will be made manifest for all to see. Also remember that your lifestyle serves as a witness to the unbeliever of who Christ is and what living for him entails. You may be the only evidence of a true Christian that someone knows and based on your genuine Christlike walk, they are likely to accept Jesus Christ as their Lord and Saviour.
Therefore soldier on in faith! Refuse to be destructed from living a sacrificially worshipful life unto God.

Poems:

A Worshipful Life

I will lift my hands in praise.
I will bow my knees in worship.
I will lay me down in surrender to
my Maker

my Master
my King.
I will proclaim the Word.
I will speak the truth.
I will tell my story of
His adoration
His salvation
His restoration.

I will give to the poor.
I will help the weak.
I will pray for the sick,
In obedience to
His call
His command
His petition.

"God has made us what we are. He has created us in Christ Jesus to live lives filled with good works that He has prepared for us to do" (Eph.2:10)

Abandoned in Worship

All honour,
glory,
splendour,
majesty
we ascribe to Him who
sits on the throne.

In complete abandon,
with vigour hot as a rod,
fervour as children of God,
we worship Him who
sits on the throne.

Resting under His gaze,
we are amazed at His
favour and grace.

Chapter 6
"One thing" to Keep the Main Thing, the Main Thing

I have had in mind author Stephen Covey's quote "The main thing is to keep the main thing the main thing" because I had a pastor who quoted it quite often in the Christian context. In the Christian context, I would say that we must know that the main thing is to keep the central focus or "the main thing" of our Christian faith the main thing.

What is this "main thing" or central focus of our Christian faith? Our relationship with God and upon this foundation, our relationship with other Christians as well as non-Christians and our God given commission to evangelise so that men would be saved.

As many know, David is one of my heroes and I will quote him when I say that keeping the "main thing" the main thing is only possible or comes naturally to us when we begin to desire the ONE THING. It is the state of our heart condition that determines whether we will activate or seek after God or keep the "main thing", the main thing.

"One thing have I desired of the Lord, that will I seek after; that I may dwell in the house of the Lord all the days of my life, to behold the beauty of the Lord, and to enquire in his temple." (Psalm 27:4 KJV).

As I quote the above, I get this sense that in fact David was stating in his own words set to music the fact that we must seek first God's kingdom; abide in Him (make Him the central focus of our lives), behold His beauty (the goodness of God in its entirety) and inquire of Him (ask Him things, to gain His wisdom, knowledge and understanding).

Living such a lifestyle, we become like David, able to have God's supernatural strength to overcome afflictions day after day. There is therefore an outflow of generosity, love and ability to forgive and accept people easily regardless of their background or what they do to us. This also enables us to see things from God's perspective.

Indeed David was someone whose life exemplified one who could do all things through God who strengthened him, likewise if we have the same conviction as David, through Christ, we are empowered or strengthened to be able to do all things (Phil 4:13).

You cannot give what you do not have, and as we are in the worst of times in terms of the works of the powers of darkness, may we stay in the place of pursuing God with more zeal as never before so that we are transformed and strengthened through His Word (the bible) and fellowship in the Spirit daily. Let us keep in mind that it is not only for our sake that we do this, but so that the fountain of living waters (Holy Spirit) within us will overflow as the works of God into the lives of our families, friends, neighbourhood and even the nation and internationally.

"The zeal of your house has consumed me" (Ps.69:9 NIV/John 2:17).
Without your zeal for God at whatever cost someone may never know God or receive Jesus Christ as Lord and Saviour, just think about that!
"And how can they hear without someone preaching to them?" (Romans 10:14 NIV).

Brethren, may we take stock of our personal lives and honestly search our hearts asking "Have I made "the main thing, the main thing" this year and past years? It is not too late for us to repent if we need to and tell the Lord that we will change our ways, preferring to cultivate an intimate relationship with Him first, rather than focusing on what we expect from Him.

Poem:

My Desire for His Things

To have all things
The Kingdom I first seek,
To do all things
Christ's strength I entreat.

One Thing I desire
is what I do seek,
to abide in Yah.
His beauty to behold,
to enquire in His abode,
His Word to savour
and rest in His favour.

One main thing I
desire is what I do seek,
to heal the sick and
strengthen the weak.
To feed the hungry the
Word of Truth,
for the way of Father to
take solid root.

Chapter 7
At the Altar of Sacrifice: What does living sacrificially for God really mean?

As believers in Jesus Christ, we have been called to not only go to the altar of sacrifice as covenanted children of God, but also to take all that belongs to us and all that we love to the altar of sacrifice with us. In other words we do not go on our own. The phrase "going to the altar of sacrifice" simply means surrendering or committing ourselves, what belongs to us; people and things we love sacrificially to the LORD.

The use of the word "altar" here is in reference to Abraham and how he obeyed God by preparing to sacrifice his son Isaac at the altar as he would do a ram or a goat. It was when he was about to kill his son Isaac that God stopped him and provided a ram as a substitute.

God then said "16..Because you have obeyed me and have not withheld even your son, your only son, I swear by my own name that 17 I will certainly bless you. I will multiply your descendants[a] beyond number, like the stars in the sky and the sand on the seashore. Your descendants will conquer the cities of their enemies.18 And through your descendants all the nations of the earth will be blessed—all because you have obeyed me." (Gen. 22:16-17NLT).

As in Abraham's case, it is evident that it is not enough being covenanted or surrendered to God as Abraham was, God requires us to covenant or surrender all that we cherish to him.

God also led me to think further about what else constitutes a sacrificial life unto God. What came to mind is the fact that our calling is to not only love God but others sacrificially.

As much as we love God unreservedly or sacrificially and we love ourselves as a result, we are also called to love others, believers and nonbelievers, unconditionally.

"Jesus replied, "…You must love the LORD your God with all your heart, all your soul, all your strength, and all your mind.' And, 'Love your neighbor as yourself.'"" Right!" Jesus told him. "Do this and you will live!" (John 10:26-28 NLT). One's "neighbour" is either a Christian or a non-Christian.

Sadly many hold back from expressing love and care towards others because of past experiences of being hurt or rejected when they had done so. Some leaders have also developed the erroneous mindset that the mark of a good leader is one who ensures they show their authority by not being too familiar with their subordinates.

Jesus ate at table with his disciples, washed their feet and allowed one of them John to rest on his bosom. Jesus did these things and more to demonstrate that in the Kingdom of God the mark of a great and true leader is one who is not afraid to demonstrate humility and love towards those they lead.

One can give all one's goods to the poor and manifest diligence in Godly service and have gifts of prophecy among others, but if one is not demonstrating the sacrificial God kind of love then one is not pleasing God. The Apostle Paul expressed it in this manner to the Corinthians:

"If I had the gift of prophecy, and if I understood all of God's secret plans and possessed all knowledge, and if I had such faith that I could move mountains, but didn't love others, I would be nothing." (1 Corinth. 13:2NLT).

Jesus who died a sacrificial death for mankind said, "There is no greater love than to lay down one's life for one's friends." (John

15:13NLT).

Jesus taught as follows "…I say, love your enemies! Pray for those who persecute you!" (Matthew 5:44 NLT)

It is worthy to note Jesus used the word "friend" in John 15:13. He also tells us to love our enemies and pray for them (Matthew 5:44). Indeed it is sacrificial to "lay down one's life" for someone who is not even blood related to us and for our enemies. It means we are willing to go the extra mile in terms of demonstrating unconditional love and kindness towards them.

Jesus was criticised by the Jewish religious leaders for keeping company with "many tax collectors and other disreputable sinners…" (Mark 2:15-16 NLT).

If we can love sacrificially despite being at the risk of making ourselves vulnerable and therefore open to criticism and rejection, then we are truly manifesting sacrificial behaviour for the sake of God as Christ did, hence affirming our love for God.

The Apostle John said, "If someone says, "I love God," but hates a Christian brother or sister, that person is a liar; for if we don't love people we can see, how can we love God, whom we cannot see?" (1 John 4:20 NLT).

Let us always remember brethren that what constitutes genuine sacrificial living before God "at the altar of sacrifice" includes but goes beyond what we normally think of as sacrifice which is the giving of ourselves, all that belongs to us to God.

In fact the affirmation of whether we are true Children of God who please God is determined by how we relate to our fellow human beings.

Therefore Brethren, when we are committed to doing all that we desire to do as living sacrifices unto God, let us remember that

God places great significance on how we conduct our interpersonal relationships on a day to day basis. May He help us in our weakness.

Poem:

Altar of Sacrifice

At the Altar of Sacrifice
I arise from the fall,
surrendering before God,
I give Him my all.

My all is giving of my heart
and that is where I start.
My all is offering what's so dear
'cause of reverential fear.

At the Altar of Sacrifice,
I give my all
to stand tall before the LORD.

My all is loving mankind
as I am loved by God
who is one of a kind.
My all is giving up my life for
friends and praying for my foes.

Always ready to pay a price,
I surrender all
at the Altar of Sacrifice.

Chapter 8
Cultivating Harmonious Co-Existence from a Christian Perspective

-The "1-2-3 Domino effect" of the Two Greatest Commandments & the Power of forgiveness

"How we see ourselves, how we conduct our interpersonal relationships are fruitful unto God, only if our relationship with God is according to His commands"

"Master, which [is] the great commandment in the law?37Jesus said unto him, Thou shalt love the Lord thy God with all thy heart, and with all thy soul, and with all thy mind.38This is the first and great commandment.39And the second [is] like unto it, Thou shalt love thy neighbour as thyself.40On these two commandments hang all the law and the prophets." (Matthew 22:36-40 KJV).

Point 1 – Point 2 – Point 3 Domino Effect

Let us ensure that the two greatest commandments are always at the forefront of our minds so that we

POINT 1 – Sustain a love-filled relationship with God through a worshipful life (e.g. bible study, praise, prayer..) which includes focus on God in all that we do and do them as unto Him.

This is the only way we can

POINT 2 – Love ourselves because it is in this place (intimacy with God) that we learn to love ourselves by understanding who we are in God and who He is to us.

As a result of Point 2 out-worked from Point 1 of the 1-2-3 Domino Effect (*whatever position we hold in the Body of Christ or society – in God's eyes a servant's heart is the mark of an obedient heart – Jesus is our example*),

We can:

POINT 3 – Love our neighbours (anyone: friend, spouse, colleague, acquaintance etc…however they treat us); this means we are able to demonstrate God's love through us to others meaning:

– we can have compassion for people,
– empathise with them,
– care about their feelings so as to be cautious how we treat them, ensuring we are not doing or saying anything to hurt them nor imposing our will or controlling them and
-treat others as we would like to be treated.

Prayer: Father, help us in our weakness so that we live according to these two greatest commandments. Thank you for answering this prayer in my life and that of my brethren. In Jesus' mighty name I pray Amen.

The Power of Forgiveness

Satan exerts himself in his attempt to ruin interpersonal relationships in general and especially those between Christian friends, spouses, ministers, work colleagues and acquaintances, because he is a sly crafty, cunning fool who will do anything to attempt to bring chaos in the harmony that is the "1-2-3 Domino Effect" of the Two Greatest commandments.

Let us take heed not to let the hurts inflicted upon us from childhood through to adulthood or what people are doing currently to hurt or upset us (it may not even be deliberate) prevent us from having or sustaining the peace we have in the knowledge that we are lovable or significant human beings created in the image of God and restored as such through Christ for His pleasure and purposes. The born-again experience opens the door for us to be healed from lies satan has said about who we are and our worth especially through others. Our healing starts with forgiving all those who have hurt us directly or indirectly and contributed to these lies about our identity and worth.

Forgiveness by God and therefore making peace with Him is conditional to our forgiving others. This is why Jesus included these words in the prayer he taught his disciples to pray ^{12} And forgive us our debts, as we forgive our debtors. (Matthew 6:12KJV). There is an assumption in this prayer that Jesus' disciples know that they should forgive others so that God will forgive them.

Jesus emphasised the importance of praying that way (verse 12) by saying: "^{14} For if ye forgive men their trespasses, your heavenly Father will also forgive you: ^{15} But if ye forgive not men their trespasses, neither will your Father forgive your trespasses." (Matthew 6:14-15 KJV).

When we forgive it means we are no longer sinning against God, for un-forgiveness is a sin. Therefore through forgiveness of others we receive forgiveness from Father God which results in our being cleansed from all unrighteousness (1 John 1:9). This makes a way for us to have fellowship with God through the Holy Spirit. Many of us have heard about how people have been healed from physical and emotional sickness when they consciously forgave others who had hurt or afflicted them.

Forgiveness is very powerful. Un-forgiveness is a decision not to demonstrate the love of God to our "neighbour" (Point 3 of 1-2-3 Domino Effect), it is therefore disobedience. Disobedience is sin and sin separates us from God. Sin prevents us from loving God with all our heart, mind, and soul (Point 1 of 1-2-3 Domino Effect). Without loving God, we cannot see ourselves the way God sees us nor love ourselves as He loves us (Point 2 of 1-2-3 Domino Effect).

Even as believers in Christ, if we refuse to forgive others, the resulting separation from God and being blinded to His truths and our identity in Him is such that we increasingly become self-dependent, self-indulgent or self-centered beings which are all marks of the fallen nature which is the image or reflection of Lucifer the fallen angel called Satan.

Lucifer's transformation from being an angel who was dependent on God and worshipped Him to become a self-centered angel manifested as pride. Self-centeredness and self-elevation are synonymous. In his pride, Satan wanted to take the place of God, to ascend the throne of God (Isaiah 14:13-15). Pride comes before the fall; indeed, Lucifer fell and anyone who chooses to deviate from living to be who God created them to be, in His image that is, is destined to reflect Satan's prideful image unto destruction.

Forgiveness is the key to overcoming Satan's attempts at creating discord, causing contention and hatred between Christians so that they do not demonstrate the love of God for one another (Point 3 of the 1-2-3 Domino Effect). This is often because when people are hurt, they are likely to fall into temptation as they are angry, discouraged, disappointed and begin to exercise thoughts of retaliation which range from either not speaking to the one who has hurt them or doing something to hurt them as well.

Your "neighbour" is not necessarily a fellow Christian and approaching them to make peace means you desire to obey God's command that you love your neighbour. Your neighbour could also

be your enemy, in relation to this Jesus taught as follows:
You have heard the law that says, 'Love your neighbor' and hate your enemy. ⁴⁴ But I say, love your enemies! Pray for those who persecute you! ⁴⁵ In that way, you will be acting as true children of your Father in heaven. For he gives his sunlight to both the evil and the good, and he sends rain on the just and the unjust alike. ⁴⁶ If you love only those who love you, what reward is there for that? Even corrupt tax collectors do that much. (Matthew 5:43-46 NLT)

The importance of forgiveness is reinforced by Jesus, expressing the heart of God on the matter, when he said that
-you must forgive those who have sinned against you not 7 times but 70 x 7 times (Matthew 18:21-22); In other words forgiveness should be a perpetual lifestyle attitude of a children of God.
-when you are bringing your offering to God and you remember that someone has something against you then you must first go and reconcile with them before doing so. (Matthew 5:23-24)

To emphasis the point about Jesus wanting us to love our enemies and pray for those who persecute us, he also said that in so doing we "will be acting as true children" of our Father in Heaven (Matt.5:45NLT). In other words we would be acting as a loving Father. God also loves and cares about that person (whether they are Christians or not) who has something against you or who has afflicted you and so should you is what Jesus was effectively saying in these aforementioned verses in the biblical book of Matthew (Chapters 18:21/5:23-24, 43-46); The phrase "..He (God) gives his sunlight to both the evil and the good, and He sends rain on the just and the unjust alike" sums God's impartiality clearly and powerfully. (Matt.5:46NLT).

It is evident therefore that the responsibility to cultivate harmonious co-existence through expressing the Love of God, lies with the disciple of Jesus and forgiveness is the key. When used therefore, this key not only opens the door to a sustained relationship of love with God, but it also serves to keep us within the cyclical realm of the 1-2-3 Domino Effect of the Two Greatest Commandments all the days of our lives.

God's Bridge of Love

You are a bridge of love for your neighbour to
traverse and progress in my love,
no more to transgress nor regress and
drown in sin.

Your neighbor is one who
favours my conditional love
or labours for artificial love.

Pour thy love upon me that
my treasury shall release plenty
into thy poverty, and
you shall see my face unveiled,
for at my gaze shall you know your worth.

When you walk with me as my bride and
talk of me with pride, as a living sacrifice,
and demonstrate my love to the loveless,
promote my Word to enemies
and use the key of forgiveness,

Then shall I draw near to you and shall
show you forth as
A shofar with the sound "GOD IS LOVE".
A passage of refuge for multitudes to
know and abide in my LOVE.

Chapter 9
Close Friends by Divine Appointment

Want Close friends made in heaven? Allow the Holy Spirit to be your best friend. If Jesus needed a close circle of friends to walk with, twelve disciples and then three who were even closer (Peter, James, and John) so do we who are his.

Seek the LORD and ask Him who should be among your close friends or in your close inner circle. Trust me, certain people do not qualify and also be warned that not everyone wants you to prosper or fulfil your identity.

When Jesus went to the garden of Gethsemane, he told some of the disciples to wait and took three with him, Peter, James, and John who were the only ones to whom he said the following: "My soul is exceedingly sorrowful, even to death. Stay here and watch with me" (Matthew 26:38).

These were the only three disciples he chose because they were destined to walk with Jesus in this manner by God. Could it be that there are people chosen by God to walk with you in different ways? Those who are mere acquaintances, close friends and some even closer? I believe so.

Not everyone should have access to your personal information. We have to walk in God's wisdom and discernment in relation to how we relate to others. Although we are called to love one another, we are not to do so to our detriment, that is not love. When we allow people to afflict us because we convince ourselves that it is because we love them and we have no choice but to accept whatever offensive treatment they give us, we are in deception. In fact fear for the person is what is keeping them bound and in enslavement to them. The two greatest commandment of God are to love God, and our neighbour as ourselves (Matthew 22:36-39). If we do not love ourselves the way God loves us to any degree to prevent other people afflicting us physically or emotionally, then we cannot love them with the genuine kind of love, which is that of God.

Could it also be that as Jesus had Judas in his entourage for only a season because he served a specific purpose only for that season (which was to betray Jesus), that likewise there are certain people in your life and mine only for a season to serve a specific purpose in that season after which God takes them away? I believe this is the case.

In my experience even as a Christian, there are people who were friends of mine, in fact the ones I am thinking of approached me so we became friends but as I grew spiritually and if I told them what God was doing in my life, they would at the time be congratulatory but then after a while appear not to want to know details of things I have birthed to the glory of God. I told them those things not to boast but because as I thought they were close friends of mine, I could share and discuss with them without reservation about such things.

I noticed they would never bring the subject up and would become scarcer in my life, failing to stay in touch as frequently as when I did not have anything significant for them to envy or feel threatened by. At times I would discern in their voice and attitude that they were not happy for me in terms of my breakthroughs or advancement to the glory of God. I thought back at one of them in particular and how she said God sent her to me in a time when I was quite distressed, and she was a great source of encouragement to me and I do believe that God sent her for not only did she encourage me but also prayed for me many times.

However when by God's delivering hand I began to change my manner of speech and attitude to one who was highly self-encouraging and unrelenting in fulfilling prophetic destiny, as well as being one to minister to her and encourage her as well, I realised sadly a change in her attitude towards me or her desire to be a consistent friend.

I never told this friend I did not need her encouragement and prayers, but something in her could not accept me anymore because I had changed. Honestly, I struggled to understand and was often hurt by certain mannerisms and attitudes that surfaced because of me speaking about what God was doing in my life positively or refusing to stay in the "poor me, pity me" mindset and attitude.

I did forgive her as God gave me a depth of understanding as to why she was acting that way, and I began to pray for her. However now having had a certain measure of God given discernment, I have stopped taking initiatives to sustain "close" friendships when I felt they are not bothered anyway to try to stay in touch or maintain closeness. In addition, I don't hesitate to let people be who start acting strange and think it necessary to pull away from me or those I personally feel led to pull away from if I discern that they don't like the new me who I know is the real healed me coming to the fore.

If a close friendship begins to fizzle out and you know your conscience is clear and you have not deliberately hurt the person or are in anyway responsible, let it end its course. I have realised that at times certain friendships are for seasons and some people cannot be close to you anymore as you advance into the purposes of God. If you dare forcefully stay in touch with them it is to your detriment especially if you discern the spirit of jealousy, envy and bitterness which is their problem not yours.

Cry out for the gift of discerning of spirits and the Wisdom of God. In these last days, whatever you do make sure you are doing all that is humanly possible in relation to godly Christian living to stay strong in the LORD and in the power of His might! The people you hang around with, call your close friends or confidants will play a great part in determining whether you stay strong and on course to fulfil your destiny.

It is only in staying close to God in the power of the Holy Spirit that you will know who God has sent into your life for mutual personal and kingdom purposes, what these are and how long for. You will also know how to interact with people as according to God's will so that you do not miss God induced mutual opportunities and blessings.

The Holy Spirit knows the wisdom and will of God and reveals them to us (I Corinth. 2). Much prayer for the fruit and gift of the Spirit will develop your nature to be as one who is shrewd as a serpent and gentle as a dove as well as one who has God's perspective on things. The wisdom and perspective of God will therefore always keep you one step ahead of the enemy.

Satan and his demons are pacing about through people and situations seeking whom to devour. The Holy Spirit should therefore be our closest or best friend first and foremost and through him we will be able to discern or know who our confidant or close friend should be. In addition the Holy Spirit will give us sensitivity as to where we should and should not go. We are therefore protected from danger and opening ourselves up to situations which include alliances that are not God's will for us.

I can testify that God has been bringing me genuine friends who are excited about and share my vision as I do theirs because we understand each other as we are equally yoked spiritually. By this I mean that the Holy Spirit is as much their best friend as he is mine.

Thank you, Holy Spirit!

Come Holy Spirit, have your way! God, we ask for a greater measure of the gift of discerning of spirits this day, to know who we should walk with closely.

We ask for God's choice of close friends in our lives who are the type of friends we are equally yoked with. Change us if in any way we fall short of the type of friends you expect us to be to others. In Jesus' mighty name we pray Amen.

Poem:

The Spirit of Truth

Truly on the road to nowhere are the walking dead masses.
With Father's truth, you're on the road to somewhere
on a daily basis.

Truly he will teach you to keep your eyes on what is vital.
With Father's truth, you will gain faith as a shield of metal.

Truly he will release you from ungodly soul-ties.
With Father's truth you will overcome Beelzebub, the
Father of lies.

Truly he will ensure you no longer waste your life in a barren state
and that you live a fruitful life to Father's taste.

Receive the Spirit of Truth.

Scriptural inspiration: John 14:26, John 16:13

"When the Spirit of truth comes, he will guide you into all truth. He will not speak on his own but will tell you what he has heard. He will tell you about the future." (John 16:13 NLT).

"But when the Father sends the Advocate as my representative--that is, the Holy Spirit--he will teach you everything and will remind you of everything I have told you." (John 14:26 NLT).

Chapter 10
Perfect Peace like a River

Receive God's Peace like a River in and through you! I pray for God's peace to flow in a never-ending manner like a river that forms tributaries into the recesses of your soul (mind, intellect, and emotions) so that you would experience a perpetual Sabbath rest of the LORD.

In this place, you will receive revelation from the LORD directly and through His Word so that out of you shall flow rivers of living waters that quenches the spiritual thirst of dry souls and hearts making a people ready for the coming of our Lord and Saviour Jesus Christ.

There is no peace like God's peace. Attempts at world peace without God as the source is just a charade and superficial for sooner or later confusion and chaos sets in. This is why Jesus explicitly distinguished his peace from that of the world when he said such comforting words "Peace I leave with you, my peace I give unto you: not as the world giveth, give I unto you. Let not your heart be troubled, neither let it be afraid." (John 14:27KJV)

As a believer in Christ you have His mind which means your mind or thoughts are focused on God. You therefore have access to God's peace (Is.26:3) which is perfect.

God speaks His peace in every situation of your life, however He requires that you do not "again turn to folly" (Ps 85:8).

To live a life in God's perpetual peace, He wants you to know that you need to be determined to overcome anxiety. How? Prayer to God concerning all things (Phil 4:6), while praying be thankful of what you have already received from him. If you can't think of anything at this moment, how about your life or your child, spouse,

family or your job? Also trust Him once you have prayed. It is only after you have done this that
"…the peace of God, which passeth all understanding, shall keep your hearts and minds through Christ Jesus."(Phil 4:7). God of Peace be with you!

Poems:

Receive the Master's Peace

Be anxious for naught and pray for what you ought.
God's peace will unfold as a treat,
if a slave to worry you are not.

Peace like a barging river shall knock down fortes of
deceit in your heart to
cause the enemy to retreat.

Peace like a fighter plane shall land on the
combat fields of your soul to dethrone the
Prince of this World, end the cycle of disorder
to commence divine order.

A peace foreign to this world in chaos
because it knows not its Master and His ethos.

Who is its Master?

He is the Prince of Peace who says to his own
"Peace I leave with you, my peace I give unto you"[1].
On a mount he sat and taught
"blessed are the peacemakers they shall
be called children of God"
So be blessed, not stressed.

Do not retaliate but demonstrate his love to haters.
Trade anger with prayer for users and live to unite dividers.

With your mates create colonies in a bond of peace
and be the harmonies to iron out creases.
Blessed vessel of peace, wrestle for the increase of God's
government and peace to have no end.

Scriptural inspiration: Isaiah 9:6-7, Phil 4:6-7, Matt.5:43-48. Quote 1: John 14:27(KJV).

God of Strength & Peace

Gracious God
speaks peace so we do "not turn again to folly"[1]
and wheels His blessed truths as on a trolley
into our hearts to make us healthy and steady.

Beloved Child,
fix your mind on God and His Christ
so you are not tricked by the anti-Christ
but able to receive God's perfect peace
"for in the LORD JEHOVAH is everlasting strength[2]"

©Deborah E. Nyamekye 18/01/2016
Scriptural inspiration: Quote 1. Psalm 85:8 (KJV), 2. Isaiah 26:4 (KJV)

A Peace Offering

Christ left you his peace
this world cannot give.
A peace from God
unknown to this world.

God calls on your heart
to know His Peace.

He pleads with your heart
to receive His Peace

As a Father, He helps you
to abide in His Peace.

Know
Receive
and abide in
what is freely given,
God's Peace.

Scriptural inspiration: John 14

Perfect Peace

Thou wilt keep him in perfect peace, whose mind is stayed on thee: because he trusteth in thee. (Isaiah 26:3 KJV)

Perfect peace is Father's reward He entreats
to mindsets stayed on Him in intimate retreat.

Perfect peace is Father's mealtime treat
so we can calmly say
"...my meat is to do the will of him
that sent me"[1]

Perfect Peace is Father's empowering gift
so we can boldly say
"I am not miffed, I labour under
divine favour!"

At Father's Banquet Table,
rewarded, we feast on meat in fervour
and drink the zeal of divine favour.

On the Mission Field,
commissioned, our works

> "Speak and preach perfect peace
> to change mindsets and speech"[2]

DISCOURSE – PERFECT PEACE

These are the quotes and the messages derived from this prophetic poem with the Isaiah 26:3 theme I felt inspired by the LORD to write:

Quote 1: This quote is from John 4:34 KJV:
Jesus saith unto them, my meat is to do the will of him that sent me, and to finish his work.

Quote 2: This quote is part of what I sense the Lord is saying. The whole message is as follows:
"Speak & preach about perfect peace to change mindsets and speech. My perfect peace, I give to those who trust me. This type of peace the world cannot give and comes from me is sustained when my people live in a place of steadfast intimacy (Father's Banquet Table) with me.

Perfect Peace cannot be sustained in their hearts if they treat their time with me as though they were employed in a part-time job; here today, gone tomorrow and only appear sometimes".
Perfect Peace, the "mealtime treat" reward enables us to engage in the "doing" (the meat) in Christ-likeness with excellence. The "empowering gift" is another way of expressing Perfect Peace as the "Mealtime treat", this time revealing the power and divine favour which gives us confidence when we engage in works for God.

Gracious Father, help us to partner with the Holy Spirit for a "check-up" on our mind's focus & trust level in our relationship with you. In this way we can repent if need be and overcome any barriers to attaining your perfect peace in Jesus' mighty name we pray. Amen.

Chapter 11
Living a Purpose Driven Life Unto God

In the Bible, Daniel did not only receive visions and dreams from God and had the gift of interpretation of dreams, he was also a man of purpose.
These were his achievements as a young man; He
-rose to pre-eminence in his own nation Israel (Daniel 1:3-6)
-rose to pre-eminence in Babylon,
a) among the wise men (Daniel 1:17-20),
b) gained power over all of Babylon (Daniel 2:48-49; 5:29) and

-obtained power over the Medo-Persian empire (Daniel 6:1-3,28).
How did Daniel, an Israelite attain so much power and authority in the heathen empires? It was because he was a man of purpose. Daniel did not wake up one day as a child of God and say, "I want to have power over nations and to be famous, I am going to do all I can to attain that goal!"
We get an insight into Daniel's no nonsense and bold "I purpose to live for God at all cost!" attitude when we read Daniel 1:8 (KJV) among other verses:
"But Daniel purposed in his heart that he would not defile himself with the portion of the king's meat, nor with the wine which he drank: therefore he requested of the prince of the eunuchs that he might not defile himself."
From a very young age Daniel purposed in his heart to be a sincere and committed worshipper of the God of Israel. He allowed God to set his goals and priorities all the time. He was not hasty in his actions but took time to be in the "Secret place" with God and to hear from Him. This is why Daniel was a man who knew his God, was bold and had favour with God and man, a foundation to build on and do exploits for God. When we develop the habit of pursuing God with all that is in us, we inevitably become His visionaries because our lifestyles scream out "Lord, I am available! Speak to me! I want to hear or see what you have to say or show me".

God is graciously raising people like Daniel today. Are we counted as one of these people? In the biblical book of Revelations, Jesus was speaking to those who are his when he said "Behold, I stand at the door and knock: if any man hear my voice, and open the door, I will come in to him, and will sup with him, and he with me" (Rev. 3:20 WEB).

These words of Jesus reveals that in addition to confessing that one is his or God's, one needs to advance in one's Christian walk to the "secret place" of His presence or intimacy with God where one receives revelation or insight into God's mind, will and purposes.
He "knocks" by offering himself to those who are his in many ways especially through the Holy Spirit that testifies of him and indwells the believer and through the Word of God which Jesus personifies (John 1).

Those who qualify to be Jesus' disciples, he calls friends (John 15:15), for unlike servants they have access to revelation of Father's words and therefore His secrets and will through Jesus, they are the ones who accept to open the door of their lives to a knocking Jesus. They accept the invitation of Jesus to "come up here" (Rev. 4:1) to abide with him closely, so that through intimacy they know God, receive His power, favour and revelatory gifts as Daniel did.
Jesus Christ also makes it clear that obedience to his will which demonstrates love for him is the key (John 14:21-26) to entering his and Father God's presence or glory. This produces a life that is purposeful unto God.

Brethren, God has not changed since the days of Daniel and if we are willing and completely surrendered to Him, God's plans and purposes will be fulfilled in our lives. If per chance you feel you have made too many mistakes and think it is too late or you are too old to get back on track, I have a message for you today, it does not matter what sins you have committed nor the quantity, nor does it matter how old you are for you can start afresh with God at any age or stage. Determine today to begin or to continue at all costs to live a purpose driven life founded on the Word of God in total surrender to fulfill God's destiny for your life.

When you do this, it means you are living in obedience to God's precious Word; These are key scriptures that one in total surrender to God abides by:

"But seek ye first the kingdom of God, and his righteousness; and all these things shall be added unto you." (Matthew 6:33 KJV),

"Trust in the Lord with all thine heart; and lean not unto thine own understanding.6 In all thy ways acknowledge him, and he shall direct thy paths.7 Be not wise in thine own eyes: fear the Lord and depart from evil.8 It shall be health to thy navel, and marrow to thy bones." (Proverbs 5:3-8 KJV).

God is willing to do whatever it takes to help us live a purpose driven life so that we are stay on course fulfilling our God given destinies. He forgives us again and again or endless times and He is a God of second, third, fourth or multiple chances. The only condition is that we acknowledge our sins and repent before Him (1 John 1:9), surrendering our lives totally to Him so as to exchange our purposes for His.

Poems:

Significant unto Self

Introduction:

I felt led to contemplate the futility and consequences of life without God. The ultimate purposeless life is one lived without God. Self-worth attained by placing one's significance in things and achievements instead of God is meaningless as is life without the God of our Lord Jesus Christ. "Meaningless! Meaningless!" says the Teacher. "Utterly meaningless! Everything is meaningless." (Ecc. 1:2).

Significant unto Self

"I am significant"
repeat this in a trance,
believe it at a glance
at your achievements
and accolades.
What is the purpose
if you have no repose
only tension with no solution?
What is the purpose
if you see the broad way of death
but are blind to the narrow way of life?
What is the purpose
if your hands are tied
and you ride on the waves
of hell and cannot tell
when Jesus calms the tide so you can walk by
faith and not by sight and be set alight to do what is right?
There is no purpose!

Intimacy with Purpose
Introduction:
The intimate relationship a Christian has with Abba Father through Christ Jesus automatically results in them having a purpose in life beyond this relationship because through it they become like Daniel as they "purpose" in their heart that they "would not defile" themselves but rather live sanctified or consecrated lives unto God. This means through obedience and surrender as Daniel they are able to know their God, receive His strength and arise in His power to do exploits. This poem is about a person who not only wants to live a worshipful life unto God "cradled" in his arms ("fat" with His blessed presence and glory) but desires more than just merely warming church pews… so to speak! He or she desires to be of use to Him for the sake of the world as a "city set on a hill", or a light that cannot be hidden.

Intimacy with Purpose

Almighty God,
dwelling in thy Secret Place I see thy face
and I am love struck and stricken by thy grace.
I have nothing in my palms to give thee as a
holy offering of alms, so I give myself to
thee as a babe cradled in thy arms.

I abide under the shadow of the Almighty,
not so that I can sleep, oblivious to the trillions
of issues in the deep, but so that I can learn to
discern thy will, be strong in the power of thy
might and emit thy light as a city set on a hill.

For Jesus said to me "You are the light of the world like a city on a hilltop that cannot be hidden. No one lights a lamp and then puts it under a basket. Instead, a lamp is placed on a stand, where it gives light to everyone in the house. In the same way, let your good deeds shine out for all to see, so that everyone will praise your heavenly Father (1)".

Scriptural Inspiration: Quote (1) Matthew 5:14-16 NLT, Psalm 91:1, Eph.6:10

Chapter 12
What it means to be an Astute Businessman or Woman of God – Trusting & Immovable.

Trusting in the Lord means that one is steadfast and therefore able to excel and is also "immovable" or unperturbed and unshaken in the face of adversity. One can face adversity head on and can even say boldly "bring it on!".

"Those who trust in the LORD are like Mount Zion, which cannot be moved, but abides forever." (Psalm 125:1 NKJV).

To convey more accurately what being steadfast or immovable entails, I would describe one who believes God is trustworthy as having the qualities of one who is astute. The ability to be astute is a product of their trust in God.

What does astute mean? It means that one has or shows an ability to accurately assess situations or people and turn this to one's advantage. Also according to the English Cambridge dictionary, such a person is "able to understand a situation quickly and see how to take advantage of it".

People often use this word in the context of secular business; "He is an astute businessman" they say. How about using it in the context of those who live a life engaged in God's business, which can be within and outside of the church? How about applying this word to people who are employed or are self-employed and as believers use godly principles that make them astute?

There is so much meaning packed within this word, astute. Synonyms of astute include: Shrewd, sharp or sharp-witted, bright, brilliant, intelligent, smart, canny, clever, discerning, perceptive, intuitive and insightful.

When we trust in God as believers in Jesus Christ, it means we surrender our lives completely to Him and live abiding in God actively through bible study, prayer and singing praises to Him.

BENEFITS OF TRUSTING GOD

One of the key benefits of trusting God is that the Holy Spirit indwelling us responds and he imparts spiritual gifts which includes the gift of discerning of spirits and wisdom (1 Corinth.12). When you have God given gifts of discernment and wisdom due to steadfast or immovable trust in God, it means that you inevitably develop the ability to have God's "eyes" or insight and perception in things the same way God does.

In simple terms you have the wisdom of God and therefore a God given "ability to accurately assess situations or people and turn this to" your advantage (quotes are part of definition of astute noted earlier). Knowing or having God's Wisdom on a matter means He will also give you the understanding for effective application; as a result you are "able to understand a situation quickly and see how to take advantage of it", again the quotation is part of the definition of astute written earlier.

Believers in Jesus Christ can know or discern the will and wisdom of God because the indwelling Holy Spirit, being the Spirit of God, knows the will or mind of God on a matter (1 Corinthians 2) and imparts it to us. As Christians, we should have at the forefront of our minds the truth of the fact that wisdom that is not from Father God through our Lord Jesus Christ is from two sources, ourselves (carnal) and Satan (including evil spirits). Therefore praying for God's wisdom to live victoriously in all areas of our lives is an absolute necessity. The apostle James says "If you need wisdom, ask our generous God, and he will give it to you. He will not rebuke you for asking." (James 1:5NLT).

Another key benefit of trusting in God is that you provoke the Word of God to work for you! You are simultaneously trusting in Jesus the Word (John chapter 1) who became flesh and dwelt among men, died, and rose again the third day to redeem mankind from sin. Jesus is described as the last Adam, the Life-giving Spirit (1 Corinthians chapter 15:45).

The Spirit of God that bears witness with our Spirit that we are children of God, testifies of Jesus (John 15:26), the Word. The abundant life of God (John 10:10) obtainable through Christ (as well as the Holy Spirit) manifests in the life of the Christian who trusts in God. The great power of enablement released by the Holy Spirit is well expressed in Romans 8:11(NLT) as follows:
"The Spirit of God, who raised Jesus from the dead, lives in you. And just as God raised Christ Jesus from the dead, he will give life to your mortal bodies by this same Spirit living within you."

Trust in God therefore inevitably results in resurrection life! Every area of one's life that is "dead" or unproductive or barren becomes fruitful. The redemptive and productive life of God is breathed into one's intellect (synonyms of astute: intellectual, brilliance, bright...). This means that as a believer in Christ, your thoughts are increasingly sanctified and become as God's thoughts.
Your creativity and entrepreneurial spirit be it in church ministry or your role in the marketplace or public sphere such as in the realms of volunteering, career and engaging in a hobby is greatly enhanced and aligned to God's will for your life. In fact God is likely to give you creative and clever (clever is a synonym of astute) ways to be an influential or fruitful witness for Christ. Jesus advised his disciples to be shrewd, another of the synonyms of astute mentioned earlier:
"Look, I am sending you out as sheep among wolves. So be as

shrewd as snakes and harmless as doves." (Matthew 10:16NLT).

God's children are rightly declared "astute businesspeople" for His sake because they trust Him. It is therefore accurate to say that when we trust in God, the truth of His written and prophetic word about who we are and what our purpose is begins to manifest or unfold. The reality of these scriptures amongst others are affirmed daily in our lives:

"By his divine power, God has given us everything we need for living a godly life. We have received all of this by coming to know him, the one who called us to himself by means of his marvelous glory and excellence." (2 Peter 1:3 NLT).

"Now all glory to God, who is able, through his mighty power at work within us, to accomplish infinitely more than we might ask or think." (Eph. 3:20NLT).

Through the power of God at work within and in every area of our lives, we not only increasingly become who we were created to be, in terms of our identity but also what we were predestined to do in terms of our destiny. This is because we have what it takes to be astute when we trust in God. Truly trusting God through His Word results in a life constantly lived in His presence. The cycle of astuteness in relation to "God's business" wherever we might be is therefore never ending. This verse that speaks of God's constant presence is a daily reality:

"As the mountains surround Jerusalem, so the LORD surrounds His people" (Psalm 125:2 NKJV).

Poem:

Trusting & Immovable

The heritage of trusting in God
is to be branded as astute.
Amiable and steadfast,
immovable as Mount Zion.

A heart of zeal is obtained,
clad in wisdom
as a quilt patched from
experiences and sown.

The ability to excel, a
covering of divine brilliance
as a shawl saved from a
furnace of chastening
and worn.

Astuteness in business,
God imparts to trusting men.
Revealed in how they
discern, assess, and walk
paths of righteousness.

The immovable shall
flourish in God's
blessedness.

Chapter 13
Who Am I? It is a Matter of Perception!

-The Street Dweller: "A Survivor, that's who I am"

Poem: The Street Dweller

They call me "Homeless"
but don't care to ask my name.
I prefer "Street Dweller"
'cause the streets are my home.

They call me purposeless
but life on the streets spell
"Survival of the fittest" that
makes me far from useless.

They call me hopeless
but I have hope as I am
streetwise.
From place to place I trek,
I know bins full of food,
and outside which shop to beg.
Bus drivers know me
turn a blind eye when I hop
on for free rides with my dog Fred.

They call me senseless
but I put to use the common
sense given by the Most High

when I look to the sky and
can tell if it shall rain or shine.
Then I know where to lay
my head; in someone's shed,
a fold up box, open air?
Anywhere as long as it
is miles away from a fox!

I am a street dweller.
Yes, among life's fittest.
A survivor, that's who I am.

Motivational Discourse & Counsel:

One who lives in a home, has an address to go to can easily think "why would one want to live on the streets! Whatever name one chooses to be called "Homeless" or "Street Dweller" does not change the fact that they are in an undesirable status in life!"

Such a thought is not necessarily malicious as most people prefer a roof over their heads, a place to call home. However as we can see from this poem, the street dweller is expressing how they perceive their situation or circumstance which is contrary to how others to his or her knowledge perceive it.

The street dweller in this poem has accepted their status as their reality. The circumstance or situation which resulted in them being as such is neither here nor there, they are proud to be homeless and making good of their life on the streets. They have learnt to survive and have dignity and self-respect. Their descriptive prose is also saying loud and clear: "this is who I am, take it or leave it!" They compel one to respect them.

A few reflections and lessons can be derived from this poem as well as words of counsel and encouragement or exhortation, here are some:

If people superficially put you in a box, assume things about you or stereotype you because of how society and others perceive or treat "people like you" e.g. your economic, social status, race or cultural background, it is actually only you and you alone who can dismantle those superficial or stereotypical assumptions about who they think you are or how they expect you to behave.

Not that you have to make a conscious effort to change their minds or attitudes about you; Your manner of self-perception, self-relation, self-definition and self-respect in relation to who you are and your circumstance will greatly influence how people treat and perceive you.

Despite being born as a member of a family you are a unique being. Unique also within one human race and within diverse racial or ethnic groups, social and economic group of humanity. There is only one you!

However if you find that despite being unique and basically your true self within and still feel unaccepted by some because of your social and economic status, nationality, race, or cultural background there is nothing you can do about it. Everyone is entitled to their opinions. However you must make sure that you stay true to who you are as a person and not be driven to say things or act in ways that agree with any false labels about who you are or what people think you are supposed to be.

People may not understand your circumstances or even know all the background experiences and elements which have made you who you currently are, but learning to connect with your true self within, loving and respecting who you are without comparison to anyone else will constantly shatter any adverse effects that negative words and actions may otherwise have on you. There is a scripture in the bible "...Love your neighbour as yourself..." (Matthew 22: 36-39)

Self-love, which includes self-respect, results in expressions of love and respect towards others. This is because you inevitably empathise, have compassion for or appreciate other human beings more. As much as you cultivate positive self-worth so too you see the bigger picture; the world is full of people who are worthy of being loved and respected as you are. It is therefore impossible for people who have a habit of debasing others or taunting and backbiting to befriend you or be among your close circle of friends.

In the context of the Street Dweller's message, being a survivor is being an overcomer from having your worth defined by how others perceive you. Whatever your status or circumstance in life, ensure that you can say like the Street Dweller:
"Yes, among life's fittest.
A survivor, that's who I am."

Chapter 14
The Battle is the LORD's: True Worshippers are guaranteed Victory in Life's Battles (2 Chronicles 20)

-A consolidated army of surrounding nations advance to attack Judah - A call to fast and pray

Armies from surrounding nations had gathered stationed to begin to attack Judah. King Jehoshaphat of Judah was terrified but he knew that the only way to overcome this fear is to seek He who can deliver and so He sought the LORD for guidance as to what to do. He ordered all the people of Judah to fast, they gathered in Jerusalem to seek the LORD's help.

Jehoshaphat prayed:

"5 Jehoshaphat stood before the community of Judah and Jerusalem in front of the new courtyard at the Temple of the Lord. 6 He prayed, "O Lord, God of our ancestors, you alone are the God who is in heaven. You are ruler of all the kingdoms of the earth. You are powerful and mighty; no one can stand against you! 7 O our God, did you not drive out those who lived in this land when your people Israel arrived? And did you not give this land forever to the descendants of your friend Abraham? 8 Your people settled here and built this Temple to honor your name. 9 They said, 'Whenever we are faced with any calamity such as war, plague, or famine, we can come to stand in your presence before this Temple where your name is honored. We can cry out to you to save us, and you will hear us and rescue us.'

10 "And now see what the armies of Ammon, Moab, and Mount Seir are doing. You would not let our ancestors invade those

nations when Israel left Egypt, so they went around them and did not destroy them. 11 Now see how they reward us! For they have come to throw us out of your land, which you gave us as an inheritance. 12 O our God, won't you stop them? We are powerless against this mighty army that is about to attack us. We do not know what to do, but we are looking to you for help."

Prophetic Word of encouragement was given.

God said through Jahaziel, before Jehoshaphat and the crowd:

"15 Listen, all you people of Judah and Jerusalem! Listen, King Jehoshaphat! This is what the Lord says: Do not be afraid! Don't be discouraged by this mighty army, for the battle is not yours, but God's. 16 Tomorrow, march out against them. You will find them coming up through the ascent of Ziz at the end of the valley that opens into the wilderness of Jeruel. 17 But you will not even need to fight. Take your positions; then stand still and watch the Lord's victory. He is with you, O people of Judah and Jerusalem. Do not be afraid or discouraged. Go out against them tomorrow, for the Lord is with you!" (2 Chronicles 20:15-17).

It is worthy to note that the prophecy was given when the Spirit of God came upon one of the men gathered whose name was Jahaziel, a descendant of Asaph. He was not a well-known prophet, yet Jehoshaphat did not reject the prophetic word, He humbly received it. God speaks through anyone He chooses, and we can only know it is God and therefore not miss His blessing if we have a heart like Jehoshaphat; humble and close to God, dependant on Him as a true "sheep" for His sheep know his voice, they recognise it is Him speaking regardless of what His voice sounds like or the vessel through whom He speaks.

As a descendant of Asaph, we know Jahaziel came from a musical family. He was from a household of musicians or worshippers and

God chose the Spirit of prophecy to manifest through him at such a crucial time when the nation was assembled waiting on God.

This ought to speak to us; our lives should be lived in such a way that we practice what we profess to be; True worshippers of God always through Christ Jesus who is our spiritual ancestor, heirs of whom we are. Being spiritual descendants of Abraham through Christ means we are partakers of the blessings of Israel (Gal 3:13-14/26-29).

When we live our lives as true worshippers of God, we are inevitably able to hear from God not just for ourselves but also on behalf of other people and even nations.

We and our descendants can be trusted by God to be His vessels to fulfil as well as convey His plans, some of which could bring great deliverance to nations as in the case of Asaph's descendant Jahaziel.

When Jehoshaphat accepted the prophetic Word of God, God gave Him the strategy of how to advance, he followed the instructions and Judah was victorious in the warfare against the great Army;

"18 Then King Jehoshaphat bowed low with his face to the ground. And all the people of Judah and Jerusalem did the same, worshiping the Lord. 19 Then the Levites from the clans of Kohath and Korah stood to praise the Lord, the God of Israel, with a very loud shout.

20 Early the next morning the army of Judah went out into the wilderness of Tekoa. On the way Jehoshaphat stopped and said, "Listen to me, all you people of Judah and Jerusalem! Believe in the Lord your God, and you will be able to stand firm. Believe in his prophets, and you will succeed."

21 After consulting the people, the king appointed singers to walk

ahead of the army, singing to the Lord and praising him for his holy splendor. This is what they sang:

"Give thanks to the Lord; his faithful love endures forever!"

22 At the very moment they began to sing and give praise, the Lord caused the armies of Ammon, Moab, and Mount Seir to start fighting among themselves. 23 The armies of Moab and Ammon turned against their allies from Mount Seir and killed every one of them. After they had destroyed the army of Seir, they began attacking each other.24 So when the army of Judah arrived at the lookout point in the wilderness, all they saw were dead bodies lying on the ground as far as they could see. Not even one of the enemies had escaped.

25 King Jehoshaphat and his men went out to gather the plunder. They found vast amounts of equipment, clothing, and other valuables—more than they could carry. There was so much plunder that it took them three days just to collect it all! 26 On the fourth day they gathered in the Valley of Blessing. which got its name that day because the people praised and thanked the Lord there. It is still called the Valley of Blessing today. 27 Then all the men returned to Jerusalem, with Jehoshaphat leading them, overjoyed that the Lord had given them victory over their enemies. 28 They marched into Jerusalem to the music of harps, lyres, and trumpets, and they proceeded to the Temple of the Lord.29 When all the surrounding kingdoms heard that the Lord himself had fought against the enemies of Israel, the fear of God came over them. 30 So Jehoshaphat's kingdom was at peace, for his God had given him rest on every side.

A summary of the qualities and actions expected of a true worshipper or a committed child of God.

With the nature of Jehoshaphat in mind, gleaned from scripture, a true worshipper has the following nature and lifestyle:

-seeks and waits on God for guidance or direction.
-prayer and fasting are a lifestyle with expectation to hear God speak.
-Even if they experience the emotion of fear, a true worshipper remembers their authority in Christ and that they are empowered by God because the Holy Spirit is within them and is guiding them. Therefore as Jehoshaphat rather than accept defeat when faced with danger in times of fear when they feel weak and helpless, they take refuge in Him (God) who gives them strength and strategies to overcome.
-A true worshipper accepts that they are called to be relational with fellow brethren for this is how God and Christ operate; Christ prayed to God for his disciples

"I pray that they will all be one, just as you and I are one--as you are in me, Father, and I am in you. And may they be in us so that the world will believe you sent me." (John 17:21NLT).

While Jehoshaphat must have trusted God to answer his prayers, he also knew that unity in prayer and fasting pleased God and so called the nation of Judah to fast and pray.

Therefore when faced with issues that concern or affect them collectively either as a church or nation, a true worshipper is not one to isolate themselves but rather join in with the brethren to engage with one another in intercession and worship before God.

Poetic Song:

The Battle is the LORD's!

The Battle is the LORD's
I shall declare it,
far and near
and shall not fear.

The Battle is the LORD's
yet He arms me with strength.
I march in awe.
Boosted and bonded with soldiers,
we march in awe.

Our strength is in
weapons from above,
mighty to pull down
every stronghold,
and cast down all powers
binding the people of God.

The Battle is the LORD's
I shall declare it,
far and near
and shall not fear.

The Battle is the LORD's
yet He gives
me strategies.
I march to war.
Skilled and schooled with generals,

we march to war.

Our strategies are wisdom
from God above,
Mighty to pull down every high thing,
and cast down all exalted against
the knowledge of God.

We are one,
from every nation,
regardless of race
association,
Rich or poor
and life's station
He calls us, we are one,
and arms us as one.

The Battle is the LORD's
We shall declare it,
far and near
and shall not fear.
We shall not fear
for the Battle is the LORD's!

Scriptures inspiring Song:
John 17:21, 2 Corinth. 10:5, 2 Corinth. 10:4, 2 Chronicles 20

Chapter 15

Exaltation of Warrior God & His Chosen Warrior King, Jesus Christ

Most High God, you have shown yourself to be a warrior God on behalf of your people, I give you praise and exalt your name above every name for you are the only mighty, unconquerable Great One!

The righteous are filled with joy and sing your praises for you sent Jesus Christ, your chosen King in righteousness and at His baptism when the Spirit descended upon him, you said "this is my beloved son in whom I am well pleased"[1] Then when the Prince of Peace, Jesus began his victorious life to take back the world you so love, while fasting in the wilderness he overcame the prince of this world.

You handed over the nations to Christ as his inheritance with authority and might over them. Indeed he, your chosen King, is the one anointed for victory and all saints through him for he said "The Spirit of the Lord is upon me, for he has anointed me to bring Good News to the poor. He has sent me to proclaim that captives will be released, that the blind will see, that the oppressed will be set free…"[2] So "Why are the nations so angry? Why do they waste their time with futile plans?

The kings of the earth prepare for battle; the rulers plot together against the Lord and against his anointed one. Let us break their chains," they cry, "and free ourselves from slavery to God." But the one who rules in heaven laughs. The Lord scoffs at them. Then in anger he rebukes them, terrifying them with his fierce fury. For the LORD declares, "I have placed my chosen King on the throne in Jerusalem, on my hoy mountain."[3]

To the kings seated on thrones entrapped in hell, the LORD warns

"Now then, you kings, act wisely! Be warned, you rulers of the earth! Serve the Lord with reverent fear and rejoice with trembling. Submit to God's royal son, or he will become angry, and you will be destroyed during all your activities—for his anger flares up in an instant. But what joy for all who take refuge in him!"[4]

Most compassionate God you said in ancient times to Israel "Don't be afraid, for I am with you. Don't be discouraged, for I am your God. I will strengthen you and help you. I will hold you up with my victorious right hand. See, all your angry enemies lie there, confused, and humiliated. Anyone who opposes you will die and come to nothing. You will look in vain for those who tried to conquer you. Those who attack you will come to nothing. For I hold you by your right hand— I, the Lord your God. And I say to you, 'Don't be afraid. I am here to help you."[5]

In these times you continue to assure your children of your love and care. "Do not be anxious about anything, bring your petitions to me with thanksgiving and I will give you peace, that surpasses all understanding"[6], "Give all your worries and cares to me for I care for you"[7] are your comforting words to your people.

"Praise the Lord; praise God our savior! For each day he carries us in his arms. Our God is a God who saves! The Sovereign Lord rescues us from death. But God will smash the heads of his enemies, crushing the skulls of those who love their guilty ways. The Lord says, "I will bring my enemies down from Bashan; I will bring them up from the depths of the sea. You, my people, will wash your feet in their blood, and even your dogs will get their share!"[8]

Oh gracious LORD, you assure us that we are "more than

conquerors"[9] through the lover of our souls, Christ Jesus; He has given the Saints authority "to trample upon…all the powers of the enemy"[10] and promised that no harm will come to us. We are raised up and "seated in heavenly places"[11] with God in Christ Jesus, exalted as he is, for through him we "are a chosen people…a royal priests, a holy nation, God's very own possession."[12a] As a result, we can show others the goodness of God, for he called us "out of the darkness into his wonderful light."[12b]

The people of God, the children in His quiver, do not fear for Yahweh is Gibbor, the Mighty Man of War, Nissi, the LORD my Banner (Standard & Standard-bearer) and Sabaoth, the LORD of the Hosts of warring Angels.

The anointed Warrior King is our Christ, the Rider on the white horse "named Faithful and True for he judges fairly and wages a righteous war"[13] and "subdues kings before him, he turns them to dust with his sword to windblown chaff with his bow, he pursues them and moves on unscathed"[14] to bring down the might of more kings and takes lands in cyclical splendour.

In victorious declaration, the King of Kings and Lord of Lords daily raises his banner and pierces his scepter of righteousness on fallow ground in agreement with the proclamation of loud voices in heaven that declare "The kingdoms of this world are become the kingdoms of our Lord, and of his Christ; and he shall reign for ever and ever."[15]

Quotes (NLT unless stated) scriptural references in this sequence: (1) Matt.3:17 (2) Luke 4:18-21 (3)Ps. 2:1-6 (4) Ps.2:10-13 (5) Is.41:11-13 (6) Phil 4:6-7 (7) 1 Peter 5:7 (8) Ps.68:19-23 (9) Romans 8:37 (10) Luke 10:19 (11) Eph. 2:6 (12a/b) 1 Peter 2:9 (13) Rev 19:11 (14) Is.41:2-3 NIV (15) Rev. 11:15 KJV.

Poems & Poetic Songs of Praise (Psalms):

Yahweh or Jehovah is derived from YHWH means in Hebrew: "I am that I am" or "I will be what I will be":

"**14** And God said unto Moses, I AM THAT I AM: and he said, Thus shalt thou say unto the children of Israel, I AM hath sent me unto you.
15 And God said moreover unto Moses, Thus shalt thou say unto the children of Israel, the LORD God of your fathers, the God of Abraham, the God of Isaac, and the God of Jacob, hath sent me unto you: this is my name for ever, and this is my memorial unto all generations.
16 Go, and gather the elders of Israel together, and say unto them, The LORD God of your fathers, the God of Abraham, of Isaac, and of Jacob, appeared unto me, saying, I have surely visited you, and seen that which is done to you in Egypt" Exodus 3:14-16 (KJV)

Yahweh Gibbor (Man of War; The Lord, the Mighty)

(Isa. 42:13/Isaiah 9:6)

Yahweh
Yahweh
Yahweh Gibbor
Mighty Man of War.

You snatched me from
the clutches of the strongman.
You took me from troubled waters.
If but for you Lord, I would have
drowned in my sorrows.
In my distress, the lights went out,
I felt snuffed out.
But you arose as a warrior!

As a warrior,
you arose!
you arose!
Yahweh Gibbor arose
and His enemies were scattered.

In fear they departed when He arose.

Blessed be Yahweh Gibbor.
Blessed be Yahweh Gibbor.
The Mighty Man of War.
The God of His people.
The helper of His people.

From generation to generation,
As dart boards, hurled darts of insults.
As prey for the hunter, hunted down.
Wanted dead or alive.
In their pain they wept and wept,
until tears became streams that
screamed "where are you Lord"?

As a warrior,
you arose!
you arose!
Yahweh Gibbor arose
and His enemies were scattered.
In fear they departed when He arose.

Blessed be Yahweh Gibbor.
Blessed be Yahweh Gibbor.
The Mighty Man of War.
The God of His people.
The helper of His people.

Yahweh
Yahweh
Yahweh Gibbor
Mighty Man of War.

Yahweh Nissi (The LORD my Banner; Standard or Standard-Bearer)
(Exodus 17:15)

Yahweh Nissi
is my Banner
A trusted Standard-Bearer
and intercessor.
He gauges the warfare
and for chastening, He
measures the right dose
of affliction to heal self
dependency and destruction.

My Standard-Bearer
prescribes a full dose of
holiness with a seal of purity
to keep at bay enemies
He has cast away.

He renders me astute as
I refuse to live by
Satan's hellish statutes.

Yahweh Nissi
is my Beloved.
His Banner over me is love.
A trusted lover of my soul,
by Him I am more than a
conqueror.

My Beloved Banner
imparts faithful promises.
As to Joshua, so to me through
Christ Yeshua the Messiah;
A perpetual warrior for my soul is
He, against the "Amalek" oppressor.

Yahweh Nissi
is victorious in battle.
His Banner is a canopy of
refuge for those who overcome
tribulation so they can fulfil
their end-time commission.

Scriptural inspiration:
Exodus 17:10-16, Song of Solomon 2:4, Romans 8:37,
Hebrews 12:5-13

Yahweh Sabaoth (The LORD of Hosts)
(1 Samuel 1:13)

Merciful God,
My heart is overwhelmed for
you came down from your majestic
throne as a man of war leading your armies
and broke through the fortress of my
imprisonment, the cage of my captivity.

You battled the hordes of hell,
the powers of darkness,
in the abyss of deception
and the trenches of affliction.

You took hold of the horned
Prince of darkness and hurled him
out of my way and lifted me up,
washed me clean and set me
along your glorious path.
Your wonders to perform.

Your acts to make known.
Your works to declare.
Your will to be done.
Hallelujah! Hallelujah!

For more information:
Bearwitness-Forerunner Ministries International

Email: bearwitnessforerunner88@gmail.com

© 2016 Light of the World-John8.12 Publishing
Wielding the Sword of the Spirit – Treasures of Wisdom Series Volume 2
All rights reserved.
ISBN: 978-09931738-9-9

www.ingramcontent.com/pod-product-compliance
Lightning Source LLC
Chambersburg PA
CBHW071312060426
42444CB00034B/1978